LEADING LESSONS

LEADING LESSONS

*Insights on Leadership
from Women of the Bible*

Jeanne Porter

Augsburg Books
MINNEAPOLIS

Also by Jeanne Porter:
Leading Ladies: Transformative Biblical Images for Women's Leadership

LEADING LESSONS
Insights on Leadership from Women of the Bible

Large-quantity purchases or custom editions of this book are available at a discount from the publisher. For more information, contact the sales department at Augsburg Fortress, Publishers, 1-800-328-4648, or write to: Sales Director, Augsburg Fortress, Publishers, P. O. Box 1209, Minneapolis, MN 55440-1209.

Scripture quotations, unless otherwise noted, are from the *New Revised Standard Version Bible*, copyright © 1989 by the Division of Christian Education of the National Council of the Churches of Christ in the USA. Used by permission.
Scripture quotations marked NIV are from the *Holy Bible, New International Version* ®, copyright © 1973, 1978, 1984 International Bible Society. Used by permission of Zondervan Publishing House. All rights reserved.
Scripture quotations marked KJV are from the *King James Version*.
Scripture quotations marked NKJV are from *The New King James Version,* copyright © 1979, 1980, 1982 Thomas Nelson, Inc. Used by permission. All rights reserved.
Scripture quotations marked NLT are taken from the *Holy Bible, New Living Translation,* copyright © 1996. Used by permission of Tyndale House Publishers, Inc., Wheaton, Illinois 60189. All rights reserved.

ISBN 0-8066-5133-4

Cover design by Marti Naughton; Cover art titled "Mother Sun" by Cathal Byrne Rich. Used by permission.
Book design by Michelle L. N. Cook

Manufactured in the U.S.A.

09   08   07   06   05   1   2   3   4   5   6   7   8   9   10

To the memory of my grandmothers—

Nellie Bell Vanlier and Lola Hutchison Porter—

my matriarchs of ministry.

CONTENTS

ACKNOWLEDGMENTS

About a year ago I was holding a spirited debate with my pastor, Bishop Arthur Brazier, and a dear friend, Bishop Horace Smith. I hold both of these men in great esteem and was enjoying our intellectual exchange discussing some of today's most challenging issues. In the middle of our conversation, Bishop Brazier said, "Jeanne, one day I want you to sit down with me and tell me what it has been like for you as a woman leader. I imagine you have some stories to tell." I was quietly awed, for no man had ever asked me that question before. Yet it is such an important question.

Our stories tell of our challenges to break into male-dominated fields, to speak our voice and struggle to be listened to, and to work with women and men who have bought into stereotyped notions of female leadership. Our stories give a glimpse into the world of business owners, CEOs and corporate executives, school principals and superintendents, pastors and denominational bishops, and community leaders and activists who have led major movements, enterprises, and causes. Each one of us has had to dispel double standards and face the double bind because we happened to be both woman and leader. And it is only in sharing our stories that men and women can come to truly understand the heart and passion of women leaders. From these stories we can extract lessons for leading and for living.

I am grateful for the women and men who have paved the way for me to lead a number of enterprises, as well as to study and write about women's leadership. The lessons of this book were learned while leading, not in a classroom on leadership development. My teachers, tutors, mentors, and midwives have been many—you know who you are, and I am forever grateful to you. In this book I have tried to share successes and failures, and to share insights I have learned about leadership from the women of Scripture, and from the men and women with whom I have worked and interacted over the last twenty years or so. These lessons are offered in love.

I am grateful to my mother, Marjorie Porter, for her nurturing, patience, and support. I have a family of strong women—sister, aunts, cousins—for which I am forever grateful to be a part.

I am grateful for a circle of praying sister friends who help me bathe this ministry in prayer: Yolanda, Carla, Wanda, Carolyn, and Leola. Whether work challenge or health challenge, these sisters storm heaven in powerful ways on my behalf. Thank you!

Then there are my co-leaders, other women with whom I partner on ministry projects to do some creative powerful things: Carolyn, Rosa, and Helen. We really have been called for such a time as this!

Thank you, Marcia, for your editing challenged me to tell the leadership stories and in so doing helped to create a book that I pray will bless each reader to tell her own leadership stories. Finally, I send a special thank you to the team at Augsburg for believing in the lessons of leading ladies and adding me to your publishing family.

SEEING YOURSELF AS A LEADER:
*Preparing for Your Insights
on Leadership*

S ome time ago I conducted a series of research interviews in a South Carolina Sea Island community working to ward off corporate resort encroachment. Large corporate entities were purchasing prime waterfront property and displacing native people and their rich culture. The community activists heading up the resistance movement wanted to enlist community members to get involved in the fight, so their first step was to train people in leadership skills.

One woman told me that, prior to the training program, she had never seen herself as a leader, she had never believed she could make a difference. The extensive program helped bolster her sense of self and changed her life. She discovered her own giftedness and learned new skills. She recognized that she had something to offer her community, and she was able to use her skills to network and build relationships with other people to help transform her community. At the end of the program, she saw herself as a leader.

There are many avenues of empowerment for women. Some women follow the contemplative path of inner healing; other women develop their problem-solving and strategic skills; others focus on creating a nurturing, organized home in which they and their families grow; still others formally develop their leadership potential. The goal of our empowerment is to become the women of influence we are called to be. Today, even though more and more of us are moving toward that divine impulse to lead, to direct, to order, to develop others, more of us need to see that we *can* lead.

A few years back, the conveners of a national pastors' and leaders' conference asked me to talk about *women* in leadership. They wanted me to define the roles of *women* in leadership—as though leadership tasks for women are different from those for men.

Leadership is leadership! The role of women in leadership is precisely the same as that of men in leadership: to lead.

Leadership entails moving people to achieve collective and mutual goals, and at some level, in different ways, each of us participates in such movement. Leaders provide vision and direction for the achievement of goals. Leaders order and structure environments for working toward vision. Leaders equip, empower, and prepare others for service. Leaders identify, develop, and place other leaders. And these tasks certainly are not confined to one gender.

Leadership is a gift given by God to humanity. God gave the ability and responsibility to "have dominion" over the earth to both male and female (Genesis 1:28 NKJV). To "have dominion" involves stewardship, trusteeship, responsibility, and accountability.

But that does not mean we are all called to lead in the same way. Each of us has unique gifts. The New Testament tells us clearly that "we have different gifts according to the grace given us" (Romans 12:6 NIV). Consequently, each of us has *unique* gifts to lead: The ways women use their leadership gifts may look different from the ways men use their gifts. Yet both are important testimonies to God calling, forming, and shaping leaders for God's purposes.

In fact, women throughout the history of God's people were called upon to lead. In the Hebrew Scriptures women served as prophetesses (Miriam and Huldah), judges (Deborah), queens and queen mothers (Esther and Bathsheba), and midwives (Puah and Shiphrah). In the first century synagogue, women served in official ministry roles and in administrative roles, such as head of the synagogue, as financial donors, as scholars, and as lay professionals. In the first century church, women served as prophetesses, teachers, evangelists, apostles, deacons, patrons, mentors of younger women, prayer leaders, and co-pastors.[1]

After the first century, women continued to lead the church in various eras, but their leadership became more and more suppressed as the assumptions and values of the outside culture influenced the church. Segregating women from leadership was not God-ordained but man-ordained. Yet women did continue to lead, sometimes in all-women communities, sometimes in opposition and resistance to unfair practices of men. Many women could not help but lead; there was within them a God-given gift, a divine impulse, to lead.

I am reminded of a young woman who came to me after one of my leadership training sessions. In this particular session we had been exploring purpose and giftedness, essential ingredients for any leader's development. This young woman asked me, "Will God call me to do something I hate?" She had my attention. "I just don't see my giftedness," she continued.

I invited her to tell me more, and as we talked, she came to the conclusion, "You know, I will never see my giftedness or potential because of how I see me." She had cut to the chase pretty quickly: Her low self-esteem blocked her ability to see her giftedness, or to see how she could use her gifts in the leadership processes of her church or community. Before she could see herself as the gifted woman God had created her to be, she had to see herself from a new perspective. What she needed—what many of us need—was a process that started with changing the image of herself that she carried around inside her. For women, healthy self-development is a crucial part of leadership development.

Fortunately, Scripture offers a wealth of insights into developing ourselves and our leadership potential. In my first book, *Leading Ladies: Transformative Biblical Images for Women's Leadership*, I presented the stories of five Old Testament women who were leaders in their own right. Taking clues from their lives, I offered four images to help women identify and discover their leadership gifts: Midwife, Choreographer, Weaver, and Intercessor.

Leading Lessons delves further into the insights that women of the Bible have to offer on leadership. There are women who show us how to partner in leadership and how to mentor others. There are women who provide us with powerful insights into leading through adversity, challenging the status quo, growing into leadership, and seeing leadership potential in unexpected people. There are women who inspire us and remind us that God created us, too, to lead. And each and every one of them beckons to us to be all that God calls us to be—women who lead.

LEADING LESSONS

- In the beginning, God gave the ability and responsibility of leadership to both male and female.
- The role of women in leadership is the same as that of men in leadership: to lead.
- Leaders are not all called to lead in the same way. Each of us has unique gifts that enable us to lead according to the grace given us. Women's leadership may not always look like men's leadership.
- The leadership gift within doesn't need to be affirmed or validated by some one else to make it "real."
- Leadership is about seeing. When leaders see the God-given leadership image inside, they can begin to see themselves making a difference.

REFLECTION AND DISCUSSION QUESTIONS

1. Have you or people around you made sharp distinctions between *women's* leadership and *men's* leadership? If so, what have some of these distinctions been? How might you address these distinctions?
2. Are there some ways you have been offering a leadership gift but have not been identifying that gift as leadership?
3. What image of yourself do you carry around inside you? Is it an image of leader?

LESSON 1

CREATED TO LEAD:
*Insights from Eve on Unlocking
Your Leadership Potential*

Study Text: Genesis 1:26-28

*As women, we are created with vast potential—includ-
ing the potential for leadership. The first account of Creation tells us that the first humans, Eve and Adam, were
created in the image of God. This lesson assures us that,
as Eve's daughters, we too are made in God's likeness.
God formed Eve and the entire created order to fulfill
God's own purposes. It is an awesome thing. It means
that we have an inherent relationship with the Creator.
It means that we belong to God. It means that we have
worth and value to the One who created us.*

☙☙

One day a colleague excitedly rushed into my office to tell me
about a message she had just heard from a "popular" radio
teacher. "This person," she recounted, "says that when men aren't
in their rightful places, God has no choice but to use women."

Apparently this was the logic the teacher used to explain the
influx of women assuming leadership and ministerial roles. The
comment disturbed me because it seemed to suggest that women
were second-string players on God's leadership team.

I countered, "Saying that God uses women only when men
don't do what they are supposed to do is to suggest that God uses
women only as an afterthought. Do you realize God called many
of us just because we *are* women?"

I thought of how God used Puah and Shiphrah, the midwives
in Egypt, as redemptive leaders to save at-risk baby boys; they
were called exactly *because* they were women. Only women had
influence to control who would and would not access the birthing
chambers during the critical period when Hebrew mothers were
giving birth. Only midwives could have saved those baby boys
from being destroyed at birth, as the law of the land required.

I thought of Queen Esther, the orphan girl of the Jewish Diaspora, who was called because she was a woman. The King needed a wife! By moving into a position where she could accept the role of Persian Queen, she was strategically placed to intercede for a nation in peril.

And, of course, there is our foremother, Eve. God created humans, male and female, and God intentionally created a woman to co-lead creation. Although "leader" may not be the first thought that comes to mind when we read Eve's story—the popular view is merely to situate her as the one whom the serpent deceived—yet, in spite of her disobedience and the consequences that followed her choice, her story affirms for us that God included a woman in the promises and provisions of creation. We need to pay attention to the underlying message of creation: God found value in both Eve and Adam. There was no valuing of one over the other. Instead, God placed female and male in relationship; together they expressed the fullness of God's image. Eve and Adam were to complement, not compete with, each other and thus bring glory to their Creator.

God blessed them and gifted them with three things: First, God gave humankind the capacity to reproduce. They were told to be fruitful and multiply. Next, God gave them the ability to fill the earth and subdue it. Humans were given the capacity to complete the natural creation, not destroy it. Finally, they were given the capacity and command to have dominion over the earth. They were to be trustees and stewards over God's manifold resources. Eve was blessed along with Adam to produce, to reproduce, and to lead.

Eve was God's first leading lady!

GETTING THE MESSAGE
Think about these things for a moment.

God knew—even dictated—our gender. God knew we were women when God called us. As God's creation, we are declared to be good, along with the entire created order. We have been given the capacity to reproduce: to make, to design, to multiply the good, to have an exponential effect on the world around us. We are created to be trustees or stewards over the resources given to us. These are liberating truths. But, sadly, too many of us really don't get it or don't accept it. Too many of us don't recognize the potential and creative power given to us at our creation.

When the first humans were separated from God, the gifts bestowed on humankind became distorted. Love became lust. Helping became enabling. Relationship became manipulation. Abundance became hoarding: Resources meant for the good of all were stockpiled by the more powerful and cunning. And leadership became domination: man over woman, wealthy over poor. Even today the giftedness within us has been perverted and distorted from years of living in a broken world. Yet the pursuing God, the God of grace, made the provisions by which humanity was reconciled back to God. And God continues to reconcile us.

It is hard for many women to accept that leadership is our birthright. Too many of us remain deceived, distracted, and discouraged. Through the love and transforming power of God, we can recover the blessings, the giftedness, and the social relationships intended for humanity from the beginning. And that includes the gift of leadership as God first intended. Yes, we are free to lead!

Yet I am reminded of the slaves in the state of Texas back in the nineteenth century. The Emancipation Proclamation was signed and went into effect on January 1, 1863. Tragically, the slaves in Texas did not learn that they had been freed until June 19, 1865. For a year and a half, they were technically free, but they did not know they were free. They could not walk in the freedom secured for them.

So it is with many of us today. We are technically free, yet not walking in the spiritual liberty secured for us. We walk around ignorant of the provisions that come with our spiritual Emancipation

Proclamation. In short, we remain bound. Our hands aren't tied, but our minds are, shackled by chains of lies about who we are and whose we are.

Recently I read a story about a *New York Times* reporter who offered to purchase the freedom of two Cambodian prostitutes from their brothel owners. Both women reportedly were in this house of prostitution against their will, were willing to tell their story to the reporter, and wanted to be free. The reporter secured the freedom of the first woman without incident; she truly wanted to be free. After the reporter negotiated the second woman's freedom price, she told him she needed fifty-five dollars to get her cell phone out of pawn. He needed to get her out of there in a hurry, so he told her she had to choose her cell phone or her freedom. Tragically, she ran back to her tiny room in the brothel and locked the door. There the other prostitutes, and even the brothel owner, begged her to accept her freedom. For the moment she chose to stay in bondage.[1]

How many of us stay trapped in things that enslave us and, though our freedom beckons, even bellows out to us, we resist making the choice to be free? Don't get me wrong; the choice to be free is not always easy. The trappings of our present bondage trip us up and fool us into thinking that things won't change, that we can't and shouldn't change. We sometimes make poor choices because we feel we have no choice.

MY WAKE-UP CALL

I remember a time in the early stages of my leadership journey where I had made my way to the top leadership ranks in a parachurch organization that was led by men. Many of them were pastors who grappled with how to interact with me as a bona fide leader, not someone in a support role, which was more typical for women in this organization.

During my time as president of one of the ministries, the board appointed an up-and-coming young pastor to be my advisor. He was a gregarious, outgoing leader who had served in my role some years prior to me. We had also dated some years before, and now his gregariousness-turned-flirtatiousness felt invasive. His continued familiarity felt controlling, and I felt uncomfortable with his innuendo, though I never expressed my discomfort.

When I faced a decision about continuing to serve as president of this ministry for the next term, a dear friend of mine confronted me. She told me of conversations my advisor held with her on a regular basis, bragging about the supposed hold he still had on me—and his other former girlfriends. She recounted story after story of his braggadocio concerning me. I suspected he needed to believe he was irresistible to women to boost his ego, and this new working relationship was bolstering his sense of self at my expense. I even suspected some of the leaders of the host denomination knew of these dynamics, but winked at his antics. I continued to go along with the game, the drama, in the name of loyalty to leadership and the institution, yet I now know that this was just another form of sexism that women in male-dominated systems sometimes face when we are seen as objects to bolster the status of men. And in many ways I participated in the sham, going along with it to get along in the system. I now know that this is called collusion. I was participating in my own oppression.

Yet the issues were deeper than just the interactions with my advisor. He was just the tip of the iceberg. He was the product of a larger system that resisted women's full inclusion into leadership on equal terms. For instance, I remember sitting around a table working to resolve a conflict with a host pastor and members of my staff. Apparently, I spoke too assertively and passionately on behalf of my organization, and the host pastor looked at me and said to me in a patronizing tone, "Now, now Sister Porter, you want your pastor to be proud of you, don't you?" He mistook my directness for disrespect and put me in my place with the implicit threat to tell my pastor that I had gotten out of line. I could not articulate the effect of his words on me then, but I felt them in the gut of my stomach. His reprimand surprised and silenced me—and in effect knocked me from my legitimate leadership place as one deserving of equal voice around a problem-solving table to that of a little girl being warned not to be too forward. That's patriarchy at its worst, and it is debilitating when not put in check. At that time in my life, I didn't know how to put it in check. I was too bound to the system and enmeshed in its traditions. But I was getting tired and sensed a need for a change.

My friend helped me make a crucial decision that was to free me and set me on a course of soul searching, deepening my leadership formation and healing. In a hushed voice, looking her directly in the eye, I said, "I have got to get out of this system. This is a sick system that is making me sick." I made a choice not to run for the presidency again. I chose to walk away from it all in order to be free. Part of me wanted to hold on to the trappings of title, office, and privilege, but more of me wanted to be free. I thank God for my friend's wake-up call and for giving me strength and courage to make one of the hardest decisions of my leadership journey.

PERSONAL TRANSFORMATION

If you are feeling oppressed or bound to stuff from the past, you know too well that the chains of lies won't simply go away. Many of us hold on to mental habits, faulty beliefs, and assumptions because they are familiar. We have learned ways of coping and dealing with the chaos in our lives because we are afraid of change. Yet God continually calls us, through reconciliation of creature to Creator, to a process of transformation.

The Greek word from which we get transformation is *meta-morphoo*. Metamorphosis—the word used to describe the change of a caterpillar to a butterfly—is derived from this same word. Just as the caterpillar experiences its transformation inside a cocoon, so our transformation begins with an inner change. We may need to change our thinking about ourselves and others. We may need a change of heart so we can believe

God and accept God's promises for us. We may need a change in our attitude or our perspective.

Transformation starts with the process of healing the places within us that are damaged from years of abuse, misuse, and under-use. Our healing includes the recovery of relationship—from selfish exchange to mutual interchange. Our healing includes the recovery of leadership—from domination to stewardship. It includes the recovery of our selves—the true persons created by God. It includes the recovery of our potential and our creative power. It is a process of recovering the gifts, the joy, the love ordained for us from the foundation of the world. It is about becoming whole. The strength of the Greek word is that transformation results in being changed into a new form. To be transformed means to undergo a complete inward change, to recover the full expression of the image of God.

Every woman who will lead others must come to grips with God's transforming work in herself. When I left that ministry leadership position, I took the first step of what was to become a profound personal transformation that brought me to the next juncture of my leadership journey, which ultimately helped to unlock my leadership potential as a researcher, writer, and advocate for women leaders.

Becoming the leader you were meant to be starts with your innermost self. Becoming a leader is not investing in a business wardrobe or changing your hairstyle to suit up appropriately. Becoming a leader is not acquiring an impressive title or the corner office suite. Becoming a leader is not climbing the corporate ladder. Becoming a leader is about mustering up the courage to walk your God-given destiny path, in order that others may follow the light of integrity that emanates from within you.

To really grasp the process of transformation, each of us has to start with where we currently are. I urge you to take a look around you. Take a deep look inside. Then consider these questions with a prayerful heart:

- Do you have satisfying relationships that build you up?
- Are you a good steward of your material resources?
- Are you able to offer your gifts and talents in your work?
- Do you express yourself freely?
- Are you participating in God's work to heal and transform those around you?

If the answer to any of these questions is no, or maybe not, then the lessons in this book from women of Scripture are as relevant for you as they were for the communities that first heard them. Their stories are part of the awe-inspiring story of God's love for humanity. They remind us that God works in the lives of women—in me and in you—and empowers us to lead in unique and distinct ways.

THE CALL TO LEADERSHIP

Yes, we know that societal traditions are deeply entrenched. We know that cultural values have excluded women from leadership. But we also know this exclusion is not a divine mandate.

It is no coincidence that we were birthed and thrust onto the scene at just this moment. Our time has come to accept boldly, courageously, and humbly the call and mantle of leadership. Too many of us fail to hearken to that leadership call because of mental models that have eliminated us from the leadership equation. As twenty-first century leaders, we need to understand that no person's skill and ability and potential can be overlooked—not because of their gender, their ethnicity, their age, or their religious persuasion. We need to collaborate with other women—and with men—to strengthen our families, to nurture and educate our children, and to continue to build the communal infrastructure of our society.

It is time to accept our rightful position to lead, to serve, and to help transform.

LEADING LESSONS

- As leaders, God continually calls us, through reconciliation of creature to Creator, to a process of transformation.
- In order to lead others more effectively, leaders must come to grips first with God's transforming work in themselves.
- Leaders must be honest about the things around and within that need to change. Leaders keep it real.
- The best leaders follow the path of transformation that God is laying out. Leaders trust the process of healing.

REFLECTION AND DISCUSSION QUESTIONS

1. What reasoning have you heard to explain why women should not lead, or should lead only in very limited ways (such as only leading other women)? How would you respond to these "explanations"?
2. What are the messages you've been taught about Eve? What shifts for you when you think of her as God's "leading lady"?
3. What areas of your life feel broken and in need of healing?
4. There is a Chinese proverb that says, "In doing anything the first step is the most difficult." If you haven't been seeing yourself as a leader, the idea of leadership might seem difficult at first. What might be a first step for you?

LESSON 2

THERE IS A BALM IN GILEAD:
Insights from the Daughters of Jerusalem on Being a Healthy Leader

Study Text: Jeremiah 8:18-22

The prophet Jeremiah gave us a glimpse into the hurt of God's daughters. This prophet looked around and saw epidemic levels of discouragement and sorrow. His people were spiritually and emotionally wounded. He seemed to ponder the irony of their having physicians who could cure the wounds to their physical body, yet there were no physicians to cure their wounded soul. Jeremiah's lament is a powerful reminder that we can bring our hurts to God and expect the balm of God's love to heal us, enabling us to lead from a place of wholeness.

杢

*H*urt People Hurt People. I was leading a seminar for a group of ministers, and I referred to this book title to make a point. I wanted to convey how necessary it is for leaders to provide places of healing before we prematurely push people into working, serving, and leading in the church. If we as leaders have not begun a process of healing, our hurts not only hurt us, but also the people we lead. Later, two of my colleagues stopped me in the hall and said, "Jeanne, that was such a powerful point you made." They both proceeded to share examples of the hurts they had seen inflicted on people by other hurt people.

While puttering around my home the next day, echoes of the previous day's conversation reverberated through my head. Suddenly, a still small voice interrupted my thoughts with: "Hurt people hurt people, but the effect of hurt *leaders* is exponential. Hurt people hurt people, but hurt leaders hurt generations." I stopped in my tracks. The voice continued. "Hurt leaders hurt organizations and systems. Hurt leaders hurt entire nations."

Defensive, over-controlling, and insecure people make defensive, over-controlling and insecure leaders—who, in turn, create rigid, overly structured, and competitive organizations, businesses, ministries, or agencies. The leader who has not sufficiently worked through her own issues will bring those issues with her into her leadership role. Just as we cannot check our skin color, gender, and culture at the office, sanctuary, or school door, we don't put our emotional, spiritual, and intellectual selves on hold while we assume a leadership role. We bring all of ourselves—spirit, soul, and body—into our leadership role. And if our spirit, our emotions, our minds, and our bodies are hurting, we will hurt those who follow us.

HURTING DAUGHTERS

Ancient Israel had been called out by God with a distinct and unique mission: to enter into covenant relationship with the Almighty to show God's purposes and plans, and to lead other nations to God. Yet the leaders of Israel had strayed far from the covenant of God and had allowed their worship to become perverted. According to Jeremiah, the nation was ill and in a state of dis-ease because the leaders were spiritually unhealthy.

The ancient nations of Israel and Judah are depicted as women, and Jeremiah used the idiom "daughter of my people" to personify them (Jeremiah 8:11, 19 NKJV).[1] This phrase speaks volumes about the tender love and care that God has for God's people—as a loving parent doting upon a cherished daughter. This phrase especially speaks to our hearts about the love of a gracious God for women—God's daughters. As "daughters" today, we too are daughters of destiny, called and chosen by God. We have been created on purpose with a purpose. Yet too many of God's daughters are hurting, broken, and unable to live out their callings to their full potential. Too many of us will miss our destinies because of deep hurts and debilitating mindsets. Too many of God's daughters are crying out, and nobody seems to be listening. Too many of God's daughters are crying themselves to sleep at night in bed by themselves or next to someone who isn't listening.

They are crying out behind closed office doors, in bathroom stalls, in the car racing down the highway to the next appointment.

We cry out with and by our actions, not just our voices. Too many of us are crying out because of deep, deep wounds and hurts inflicted by outside forces at many levels. Sometimes our wounds have been caused by our breaking of covenant with God; but many of our wounds have been inflicted by others breaking covenant with us. These wounds leave scars, gashes to our hearts and our souls, and have damaged our very sense of self. Some of us have been repeatedly hit with verbal insults. Others of us have been accosted by sexual, physical, and emotional abuse. Still others of us have been rejected by friends or other loved ones. Some of us have been rejected by societal standards because we don't live up to some contrived notion of beauty or glamour. Some of us have been abandoned by people we loved dearly and counted on for support. Some of us grew up in chaos and emotionally checked out because we could not bear any more wounds.

Whatever the cause of your wounding, if you are like many of us, you have developed ways of coping with the pain and compensating for those who hurt you. You have learned to deal with pain. You have learned to walk around in the pain. You have gotten comfortable with the pain.

A few years ago I developed large bunions on both of my feet, and my feet seemed to hurt all the time. They throbbed when I walked around for too long in shoes that grew tighter with every step. One particular Saturday I had been conducting a morning workshop and had been standing for a few hours in heels. When I got home, I walked into my bedroom, kicked off my shoes, and exclaimed, "Whew, I am tired of walking around in pain!" Those cute but too tight pumps had to go.

As the shoes went hurling across my bedroom floor, I heard a quiet voice deep within my spirit: "I didn't create you to walk around in pain." That message cut me to the quick. I was not created to walk around in pain, and the Spirit was not referring just to the bunions on my feet. I had developed "bunions" on my heart. These calloused, hard parts of my heart protected me from being hurt again.

God showed me that these fortified walls around my heart were also keeping God's love from penetrating to heal the very wounds I had been trying so desperately to protect. The walls around my heart were keeping me defensive and isolated, unable to open up to the healing touch that came from God and from healthy relationships.

It is natural to want to avoid pain, to develop ways of not being hurt again. But many of us develop ways of dealing with and taking the pain that are hurtful to us. As an African American woman, I thought taking the pain, and living with the pain, was part of being a strong Black woman. I saw my mother do it, and my grandmothers do it: ignore the pain and keep on working, serving and doing for others. Later I learned that my Latina sisters were sold the same bill of goods: "Be strong Brown women." My European American sisters were told a similar message: "You have to be strong." My Asian sisters were told a similar message: "Save face and keep the pain in its place."

It seems that many of us learned a number of strategies to deal with the pain in our lives. We may fabricate or concoct a reality to fool ourselves. We may tell lies to ourselves and to each other. We may pretend we are not hurting. We may tell lies that veil us from the truth, lies to avoid facing the pain and admitting we need help.

Some of us learned to anesthetize the pain to keep us from feeling the pain. We eat, we drink, we do prescription drugs, we tear others down—all in an attempt to feel better about ourselves and silence the nagging feelings of anguish and loneliness deep in our hearts. Someone told me once, "You can't heal what you don't feel." Our hearts are sick and in need of healing.

Some of us keep busy to ignore the pain. We tell ourselves it will go away if we just work harder. We work to prove to others—and to ourselves—that we're worthwhile, all the while crying inside and wondering why we don't feel better. To quiet the throbbing cries of our lonely hearts, some of us work extremely hard to earn someone else's love. We learn too late that we can't make somebody love us. We find out the hard way that we can't demand love: Love that is coerced is not love.

With the words Jeremiah spoke centuries ago, we lament: "My joy is gone, grief is upon me, my heart is sick (8:18 NRSV). We join Jeremiah in asking, "Is there no balm in Gilead? . . . is there no recovery for the health of the daughter of my people?" (8:22 NIV).

HEALTHY DAUGHTERS

The daughters of Jerusalem cry out to us: Even today there is recovery for the health of God's wounded daughters. God wants us to be healed, healthy, whole, and complete. Jeremiah wondered aloud where to find the healing balm for the hurts of God's people, but he never stopped believing. We too can believe in God's desire to heal us. Jeremiah's certainty that God would heal was powerful: "Heal me, O Lord, and I shall be healed" (Jeremiah 17:14 NIV). We too can be certain that God's message of healing is for us: "I will restore you to health and heal your wounds" (Jeremiah 30:17 NIV). We can embrace the prophetic vision of healthy daughters dancing and rejoicing because of God's restoration (Jeremiah 31:13).

The beginning of our healing starts with three powerful truths that can erase the old tapes in our heads that blare out messages of self-contempt and self-loathing. When we can accept, embrace, and internalize these truths, God's love can change self-hate to self-love.

⊙⊙

Truth 1: God loves you with an everlasting love: "I have loved you with an everlasting love" (Jeremiah 31:3 NIV).

God loves each of us individually, uniquely, eternally, and unconditionally. When we fail to internalize God's love, we end up trying to handle things for God. Perhaps we really don't believe God loves us and has our best interests in mind. Yet like Jeremiah's message to his people, we have to accept that our misguided ways of coping with our pain provoke God. They are insults to a loving God who dispenses grace to heal us, who hovers over us, and is near us to help. Our dis-ease concerns God. God desires and orchestrates our total healing—the transformation and renewing of our minds (Romans 12:1-2), and the restoring of our spiritual, emotional, and physical health (1 Thessalonians 5:23). God's love has the power to penetrate the sores of our soul to bring healing and restore us to health.

ॐ

Truth 2: God wants you healthy to carry out your purpose: "For I will restore health to you, and your wounds I will heal" (Jeremiah 30:17 NRSV).

Healthy leaders lead on purpose. Unhealthy leaders seem to continually sabotage their purpose and destiny. In order to avoid these self-defeating patterns, we need to see our need for help, change, or support before we can be effective in leading others. The good news is that the promise of healing is ours. We can embrace Jeremiah's ancient vision for spiritual health today. God wills to heal us and facilitate our recovery. And God's healing is not superficial; God's healing is radical. Contrast God's remedy with that of false healers, whom Jeremiah described as those who "healed the hurt of the daughter of my people slightly" (Jeremiah 6:14, 8:11 KJV). God's healing goes deep and knows no bounds.

ॐ

Truth 3: God has a plan for your life: "For I know the plans I have for you," says the Lord. "They are plans for good and not for disaster, to give you a future and a hope" (Jeremiah 29:11 NLT).

As leaders, sometimes we get caught up in trying to plan every detail of our lives, businesses, or ministries, only to find ourselves getting stuck when we realize the short-sightedness of our own planning. The issues within us that have been left unchecked and unsubmitted and not yielded to God's healing touch prevent us from being who God ordained us to be. They prevent us from doing all that we can do to live out God's awesome plan for our lives. Each of us must come to believe in the hopeful future God has in mind for us.

HEALTHY LEADERSHIP PRACTICES

A recent incident caused me to come face to face with these three truths. Helen, a dear friend, asked me to join her in building a management team for a health and wellness company she had just joined. She had come back from the January launch ecstatic about the possibilities of the company and exuberant about the health product qualities. Her enthusiasm was contagious, and I agreed to join her. At the time I was recuperating from major surgery, and the wellness concept appealed to me. I committed to put in a certain number of hours a week toward this venture, in addition to running my full-time consulting practice. My plan was to build my team primarily by phone during my two-month recuperation period, and let the team continue to grow once I had to hit the road again seeing my clients.

The plan started out well: I loved the company's products, and very quickly I built up a customer base. But after my recuperation period, my consulting and speaking schedule picked up considerably. I had landed a couple of new clients who were keeping me hopping, and I found myself on the road for nearly six straight weeks. I had no time to tend to my side venture, and it seemed to fizzle before my eyes. Meanwhile, Helen continued to focus on building her team and had recruited four or five strong business builders. She set up weekly conference calls for the team members to connect, share ideas, and learn about new product features. I faithfully attended these calls during the period of recovery from my surgery, but as soon as the pace of my consulting practice increased, I began to miss the conference calls.

By about the fourth month, Helen started calling me to let me know that my customers were not ordering. I knew what the problem was: After speaking at conferences and tending to clients, I had no energy to call customers. I didn't feel like holding their hands, and Helen's follow through was beginning to annoy me, so I started avoiding her. As my side business steadily dwindled, hers continued to grow, and I felt worse and worse about the process.

After a few months of this cycle, she and I had a serious talk and agreed that this business, as profitable as it was for others, may not have been for me at that time. On top of my other obligations, I did not have the time for a side venture. I had taken on more than I could handle—an old pattern of coping that periodically surfaces in me. My over-functioning almost allowed a failed business attempt to draw a wedge between me and a lifelong friend, and the failed enterprise left me questioning my own leadership. It was time for me, like the daughters of Jerusalem, to assess the health of my leadership. Some serious prayer and soul searching revealed that some old hurts and negative mindsets were pushing me into hyper levels of over-achievement and poor judgment. I needed a healing balm to soothe and quiet my soul.

My friendship with Helen was never totally in jeopardy, but I did need some space to gain perspective on what had happened. After a few months we spent time talking about and reflecting on this experience, and I had to admit that I exhibited a number of unhealthy leadership practices that may have doomed my business from the start. I had to remind myself that God really does love me—and consequently wants what is best for me. I don't have to work so hard to prove my worth. I had to remember that God wants me to be healthy to carry out my purpose—my level of activity had not been healthy and eventually would have sabotaged my purpose. And I had to remind myself that God really does have a plan for me—and that I could stop my compulsive tweaking of the plan. God had to show me how to turn my unhealthy practices into healthy leadership practices. Through this experience, God helped me to learn the importance of purpose, timing, and trust to healthy leadership.

PRACTICE 1: HEALTHY LEADERS LEAD ON PURPOSE.

The healthy leader must be clear on her purpose and understand that the commitments she makes, the enterprises she builds, and the teams she leads must be consonant with her purpose. Each of us is gifted in ways that help us fulfill our purpose; in fact, our gifts and experiences often give us a glimpse into our God-given purpose.

Part of my friend Helen's purpose is to build organizations that are financially successful so she can sow those seeds back into the community. She is gifted at building teams and at running large profitable organizations, and her venture with the wellness company was a good match of her gifts and purpose.

My purpose is to help build people and processes, and I am a gifted facilitator. But I failed to connect my purpose to this side venture. I saw it as an add-on, not as an organic part of my purpose. When competing priorities arose and I was pressed for time, I could not give the new activities the attention needed to sustain them. Additionally, as Helen's organization grew, I began to feel badly about my inability to build my part in the same way she did—all the while overlooking the powerful things that were happening for me with my own business and church clients. I had begun to covet Helen's leadership and dismiss my own. I learned that, as a leader, what I do must be intimately connected to my purpose.

The healthy leader leads on purpose and values the gifts she possesses to accomplish such purposeful leadership.

PRACTICE 2: HEALTHY LEADERS UNDERSTAND THEIR SEASON TO LEAD.

Any meteorologist will tell you that a season is a period or space of time in which similar weather patterns persist. In North America where I live, we have four seasons (except in Chicago, my home, the seasons seem to collapse into two—winter and summer!). With modern technology we are not as tied to the seasons as our forebears from a more agrarian time were, yet even now we order our lives around the seasons. We have different activities for summer, fall, winter, and spring and, for me, biking on the Lake Michigan bike path near my home is a lot easier done in July than January.

Healthy leaders come to understand a similar principle: Spiritually, a season is an appointed time to carry out an activity or to fulfill a purpose. In biblical Greek, *kairos* is a season of strategic significance. It is a season that is set forth by God to accomplish God's purposes: "There is a time for everything, and a season for every activity under heaven" (Ecclesiastes 3:1 NIV). In my work with Helen, I had misunderstood the season for my leadership. This was a season for me to build my consulting practice. Instead, I became distracted with a new venture, trying to force fit it into my currently full schedule.

When we miss our season and overload our calendar, we suffer, and those we serve suffer. We suffer because we miss the chance of fulfilling our true calling. During the time I was trying to do two businesses at once, I was invited to speak before a group of pastors to whom I could have introduced my first pastors' training manual. Instead, I diverted the time needed to finalize the manual into securing customers for the wellness company. I ended up missing an opportunity to share a helpful leadership tool with church leaders. The leader who misunderstands her season is like the Chicagoan trying to plant flowers in her garden plot in February. The ground is frozen and the winds too harsh; conditions are just not right to break ground for a fruitful venture.

PRACTICE 3: HEALTHY LEADERS TRUST GOD IN THE PROCESS.

Healthy leaders are called to make judicious plans using the best information available at the time. Yet at some point the healthy leader has to have faith—faith in God to secure her future while she does the best she can making wise decisions day to day.

When I first joined Helen's business, I was approaching middle age and becoming more and more concerned about securing my retirement. Fear of an uncertain economic future clouded my judgment. I saw an opportunity to build wealth quickly, and I made a decision based on fear. My fear caused me to temporarily suspend my core God-given purpose in favor of an equally good process, but one that was ill timed for me.

I had to learn to trust that God was at work in my process of building a consulting practice. I began to notice that God was helping me network and secure consulting contracts, build relationships with clients, identify organizational and team needs, and develop products and services to address these needs. The process I was in was working, but it was taking some time for me to realize its long-term success.

The healthy leader cannot operate out of fear. She has to trust that she is in process—be it a business process, a development process, or a relational process. She has to learn to wait and give the process—and God—time to work.

☙❧

The promise is ours. In spite of the fact that our wounds hurt us, in spite of the fact that they surface when we least expect them, in spite of the fact that issues we thought were resolved periodically pop up and affect our leadership, the cries and prophetic hope of Jeremiah rings loud for us: God's healing balm is available to continually heal us. We can embrace Jeremiah's vision for spiritual health today. We can indeed be assured of God's love, purpose, and plan. We can walk in the assurance of God's grace.

Truly the daughters of Jerusalem cry out to us: There is recovery for the health of God's daughters. We can lead from a place of wholeness.

LEADING LESSONS

- Leaders are created on purpose with a purpose.
- Leaders bring all of themselves—spirit, soul, and body—into their leadership role. Leaders whose spirits, emotions, minds, and bodies are hurting will hurt those who follow.
- Pain is not meant to be a permanent condition. Leading from a continued place of pain is not leadership—it's suicide.
- God's love has the power to penetrate the souls of hurting leaders to bring healing and restore their health.
- Healthy leaders trust that they are in process. They learn to wait and give the process—and God—time to work.

REFLECTION AND DISCUSSION QUESTIONS

1. What type of pain are you holding onto and walking around in? What are some of your unresolved emotional or relational issues?
2. In what ways has this pain affected your life? Your leadership?
3. Take a moment to identify some of your unhealthy leadership practices. What are things you do as a leader that reflect some unhealed hurts within?
4. What are ways you can use the three foundational truths in this chapter—God loves you, God wants you to be healthy, and God has a plan for you—to develop healthier leadership practices?

LESSON 3

FROM WATERPOTS TO WORSHIP:
*Insights from the Woman
of Samaria on Empowerment*

Study Text: John 4:5-42

The people of her town most likely had dismissed her, counted her out. Yet after a "little talk with Jesus," this weary woman at a well was transformed into a well woman. She was freed to accept her own reality and to walk in God's accepting, non-judging love, and she became empowered to lead the people of her town to the Christ. That's our promise also: to become well women, women who are accepted, loved, and empowered to lead. In fact, our ability to be an effective witness of God's transforming grace is directly related to our ability to be honest about ourselves and God's transforming grace at work within our lives.

ဢၕ

I t must have started off as an ordinary day, the day this now infamous Woman of Samaria encountered Jesus at Jacob's well in the town of Sychar. Drawing water from the community well was standard fare. The woman would no doubt use the water for washing, cooking, cleaning, and drinking. Focused on her task, she was interrupted by a stranger who asked her to give him something to drink.

This story, however, is deeper than a local woman giving a traveling stranger a drink of well water. Let's face it: Jesus could have quenched his own thirst. In fact, the biblical text never records him actually receiving his drink of water. No, Jesus did not see her as an object to fulfill his needs but as a subject in need of his objective perspective. He saw the yearning, longing, spiritually thirsty woman and knew only God's steadfast, refreshing love could fill her. The empowering Savior saw her, acknowledged her, and entered into authentic dialogue with her. Truly our empowerment starts with an authentic encounter with the God who sees the real us.

WILL THE REAL YOU PLEASE STAND UP?

What others say about us may say *some* things about who we are, but how we describe ourselves says the most about our identity. When Jesus asked the Woman of Samaria to give him something to drink, she responded, "How is it that you, being a Jew, ask a drink of me, a Samaritan woman?" (John 4:9 NKJV). Her self-identification gives us a glimpse into how she saw herself. Her words also speak volumes about how her society saw her. According to the standards of her culture, this woman would have been considered powerless. The writer John does not even give her a name; she is identified merely by her country. She was "just" a woman—an outsider in a male-dominated culture. She was a Samaritan, Jesus was a Jew, two ethnic groups in tension at that time. She probably was a working woman of a servant class. We have no reason to believe she held financial or material power. She lived on the margins of gender, ethnic, and social power.

Think about it for a minute: How do you answer the question, "Who am I?" For many of us, our sense of identity is based on our looks, our body image, size, shape, our hair color or complexion. For some of us, our identity is based upon our possessions. We think we are what we own: "I am a homeowner," for instance. For others of us, our identity is based on our job: "I am a teacher"; "I am a lawyer"; or "I am an administrative assistant." Some of us identify with our social circle: "I am a member of First Church" or "I belong to Society for Women in Management." Others of us base our sense of self on our role. Not only do we say "I am a mother" or "I am a wife," but our entire sense of being depends on these roles.

Though many of these identifiers might be laudable, they prove to be false bases for our identity because they do not represent our true self. What happens when our looks fade, or we lose our possessions or job or social standing? What happens when our role in our family changes? When the labels we give ourselves no longer apply, we may feel stripped of our identity—even our value.

I am reminded of mothers who seem to lose their identity when the children they devoted their entire lives to leave home. I heard one empty-nest Mom say, "I don't know what to do with myself now. My whole reason for living was to care for my children."

I also think back to the onslaught of downsizing that took place in the early 1990s. Women (and men) who had come to define who they were by the nameplates on their office doors and desks were stripped of their titles and status. They seemed to flounder, no longer feeling a sense of worth and unable to recapture the importance that once accompanied the jobs that were eliminated with a decisive executive order. A truly empowered person understands that what she does for a living is not who she is. Becoming aware of how you see yourself and aligning your self-definition with your Creator's definition of you is the first step toward empowerment.

A DEEP THIRST

What had started out as a conversation about *well* water transitioned into one about *living* water:

> If you knew the gift of God, and who it is that is saying to you, "Give me a drink," you would have asked him, and he would have given you living water . . . those who drink of the water that I will give them will never be thirsty (John 4:10, 14 NRSV).

Without any preliminaries, Jesus brought the Woman of Samaria face-to-face with her spiritual reality. He knew she thirsted for significance. He also knew that she may not have been aware of her deep thirst. Many of us remain unaware of the source of our deepest longings and yearnings. We deny our deepest pain, pretend things don't bother us, and work hard to find significance in our looks, possessions, jobs, or social standing. We search for significance until we have an encounter with the Christ, as the

Woman of Samaria did, and are confronted with the truth of our lives: Our core identity is spiritual, not material.

Jesus also understood that, like many of us with thirsty souls, the Woman of Samaria was looking for love in all the wrong places. It appears from the text that she had attempted to quench her thirst through men. She had tried to fill the void in her heart with husband after husband, the way a child grabs for a new toy after discarding the old one. In her culture, however, she was the one most likely discarded. We hear only one of the results of her pattern of unhealthy relationships: five former husbands plus one current man.

Her history no doubt affected her reputation in the community. Most likely she saw herself as a person with little value and no power, and I'm sure the rest of the community dismissed her. Even today some denounce the Woman of Samaria for her supposed lewd lifestyle. However, the text does not give much insight into the facts of her five previous marriages. Perhaps she had lost five husbands. Perhaps she was caught in the web of a levirate marriage—an ancient custom that required a deceased husband's brother to marry the widow in order to perpetuate the dead husband's lineage. Whatever the case, these relationships did not satisfy her deepest thirsts for significance. Thank God for the seventh man who came into her life.

It is important to note that, as Jesus pointed out the facts of her past relationships, he did not judge her or condemn her. He created a conversational space in which she could explore more in-depth spiritual truths. He was concerned about the total woman, especially her spiritual health. In her encounter with Jesus, the Woman of Samaria experienced a truth moment, an "awakening" or "aha" moment.

Truth moments propel us out of denial. When we're in a tough situation, many of us try to remain in denial by not accepting the truth about the situation or by not accepting reality. Some of us deny reality by pretending certain events did not happen, or we creatively weave our own interpretations of events. As with the

Woman of Samaria, the void inside of us may manifest itself in different ways: suffering through a series of failed relationships, continually moving from job to job, or taking on more projects than we can handle. These ways of denying truth signal our need for truth moments. That is what the Woman of Samaria experienced in the presence of Jesus.

KEEPING IT REAL

When Jesus confronted the Woman of Samaria with the truth about her life, she must have been astounded. She had never even met this man before! Yet Jesus used this opportunity to gently lead her to a deeper spiritual truth, transitioning the conversation this time from waterpots to worship.

He told her, "God is Spirit" (John 4:23 NKJV). Spirit is the authentic, dynamic, creative, and sustaining force of life. Spirit is not material but brings life to material beings. Like the wind, the Spirit blows, and like a brooding hen, the Spirit hovers. Jesus told the woman that those who worship God must do so from their spirit—the deepest essence of their being. Such honest seeking after and loving God propels us toward the truth of God. And in grasping the truth of God, we can begin to grasp the truth about ourselves. Jesus called this ability to grasp and be grasped by God "worship in spirit and truth" (John 4:23 NKJV).

Jesus assured the woman that worship was not about position—place or region—but a perspective of the heart. Worship is the process by which our spirit is connected to the Spirit of our Creator. In worship, the Spirit of Creation, the God of life, hovers over the chaos of our souls to bring order and call forth life and healing. True worshipers worship God from an integrity-filled and authentic heart—"in spirit and truth" (John 4:24 NKJV).

Now, I believe many of us get the "worship in spirit" part down pat during our times of gathering together. Our liturgies and worship services are spirited and touch our hearts. Some of us dance and shout, clap our hands; some of us clasp our hands together in contemplative silence and meditation; some of us sing from hymnals and pray from prayer books; and some of us sing in the Spirit and pray in tongues.

Yet too many of us miss the "worship in truth" part. When the service is over and the "Spirit dies down," we take off the spiritual suit and don another role. We have mastered playing the game, pretending to be things we are not just to please people. In truth, our source of empowerment comes from a *lifestyle* of worship, walking daily in spiritual integrity and authenticity. This means getting real with God, telling God about our hurts, our pain, our anger, our disappointments. When we make getting honest with God a priority in daily worship and prayer, the refreshing streams of the Holy Spirit wash over us. And when we get real with God, we can keep it real with ourselves and with others.

I distinctly remember a time of having to be confronted with my own reality. I had been climbing the corporate ladder while simultaneously climbing the ministry ladder. My weeks were spent traveling across the country providing organizational development and training services to executives and managers of the Fortune 100 Company that employed me, and my weekends were spent leading various youth ministries in my local church and in our state and national affiliates.

I was living the so-called glamorous single life of a jet-setting professional. By age thirty-one, I reported directly to the president of a major division of my corporation and was being considered for other executive positions across the country.

But one day it all came crashing down upon me after weeks of grueling travel. Back in my downtown office, I shut the door and found myself sobbing uncontrollably. I called my aunt who had discerned a call to ministry in me years ago. I had to get real—I could no longer keep up this pace. I could no longer pretend that my striving for achievements and success were filling the void within. In fact, I had to admit that the two ladders I was climbing were not on parallel paths. To the contrary, they were growing further and further apart, and I could no longer balance my feet on the rungs of two competing ladders. I could no longer lead two lives, separate and unequal.

In one afternoon, the Woman of Samaria had a life-changing conversation with Jesus. For me, it took a series of life-changing conversations that traversed a number of years and included many steps of faith: graduate school, university teaching, corporate consulting, and seminary. As I got real with myself and my God, a deep sense of purpose and calling became clearer. My "worship in truth" brought a professional and personal integration that emanated from a deep place of integrity within.

A WELL WOMAN

Prior to her encounter with Jesus, the Woman of Samaria is depicted as a lone sojourner, plagued by past relational failures. Yet after her encounter, she led numerous men and women of her town to Christ. Leaving her waterpot, "the woman went back to the town and said to the people, 'Come, see a man who told me everything I ever did'" (John 4:28-29 NIV). Her testimony was simple but effective. She had become a well woman: a woman who could defy stereotypes—and her past—to walk in her calling.

The people of the town flocked to Jesus because of the woman's words. In fact, John highlights the effectiveness of her witness: "Many of the Samaritans from that town believed in him because of the woman's testimony" (John 4:39 NIV). John likened the people's eagerness to respond to the woman's witness to wheat that is ripe for harvest.

The Woman of Samaria had been empowered to lead! Jesus had helped her make peace with her past and accept the peace that comes from being in authentic relationship with God. She had become a well woman with a strong witness.

Like the Woman of Samaria, I laid down my waterpot of career ambition, status, and ladder climbing. That empowered me to move on to a place that ultimately led to the forming of my ministry-based consulting practice. I now incorporate spirituality into my consulting, and I serve corporate, churches, and community groups with a passion that comes from a deep and settled knowledge of who I am, and whose I am. I lead now from a sense of purpose and not from a fixed position or misleading title.

A well woman accepts her past but does not let it keep her stuck or prevent her from moving forward into her future. A well woman learns the lessons that good and bad experiences can teach her. A well woman keeps walking, rejoicing in the grace that has been extended to her. A well woman keeps walking, leaving her waterpot of hurts and guilt and shame behind. A well woman keeps walking, sharing the good news of Christ with other people, leading other women and men to the truth.

Isn't that really the goal of Christian leadership, to lead people to a deeper relationship with God so that they come to discover their own truth and unlock their hidden potential? As our relationship with Christ is strengthened through "worship in truth," we become empowered to share the message in our own unique ways. An empowered leader comes to know who she is—and whose she is—and taps into the God-given power within. An empowered leader is comfortable with her own style and understands her strengths and weaknesses. An empowered leader takes time to explore her sense of self to ensure that her core identity is based on spiritual truths.

Perhaps, like the Woman of Samaria, you are at a crossroad—the intersection of your past and your future. Perhaps the pain and disappointments of your past have been your constant traveling companions. Perhaps it is your time to come to the well, acknowledge your spiritual thirst, and draw from the Living Water. May this woman's story of healing and empowerment encourage you to have that encounter with Jesus about your own transformation.

LEADING LESSONS

- Leadership empowerment starts with an authentic encounter with the God who sees the real person.
- Leaders have to make peace with their past before they can move forward effectively in their calling.
- Empowered leaders understand that what they do for a living is not who they are.
- Spiritual leaders drink regularly and often from the well of Living Water.
- When leaders get real with God, they can keep it real with themselves and with others.
- Empowered leaders come to know who they are—and whose they are—and tap into the God-given power within.

REFLECTION AND DISCUSSION QUESTIONS

1. How do you define yourself?
2. In what ways has your role identified you? In what ways has it kept you from developing your leadership potential or helped you develop your leadership potential?
3. Have you ever had a "truth moment" when you knew something *had* to change? What happened?
4. In what areas of your life today do you need to be more honest with yourself and with God? What steps could you take to develop a lifestyle of "worshiping in truth"?

LESSON 4

PUTTING AWAY THE IDOLS:
Insights from Rachel
on Discovering Value Within

Study Text: Genesis 29:1-35,
30:1-24, 31:1-21, 35:1-4

Rachel, the one who led her father's sheep down a dusty trail to a dusty well, leads us to a deeper understanding of how our culture, society, family, and religion shape our sense of self and hence our sense of our leadership potential. Leadership development is ultimately about self-development. In fact, the most effective leader is the woman most comfortable with her self. She has been able to separate her self from the construction of myths and expectations projected onto her by others. Ultimately, Rachel died in childbirth, delivering one of her dreams. May you reclaim the true you in time to give birth to your dreams.

❦❦

The story starts out innocently enough. Rachel was a shepherdess who daily led her father's herd to the community well. One day while leading her flock, she met a distant relative named Jacob. What she didn't know was that Jacob had journeyed to her country seeking a wife among his mother's people. When he saw Rachel, he was moved to tears. Jacob's dream of finding his people and a wife was coming true before his eyes. As soon as he explained to Rachel who he was, she ran to tell her father, Laban, of the kinsman's arrival.

Now Laban had another daughter named Leah, who is described as having weak eyes (Genesis 29:16-17 NIV). In contrast, Rachel is reported to have been "lovely in form, and beautiful" (Genesis 29:17 NIV). The writer of this passage seems intent on lifting up the differences between these two sisters. The valuing and devaluing of women based on physical attributes did not originate in our twenty-first century commercial culture! Labeling women, which puts us in categories that create competition among us, is a practice as ancient as the human story.

Smitten with Rachel, Jacob offered to work seven years for her bride's money, as was the custom among many ancient cultures. However, it wasn't until *after* the wedding feast that Jacob realized he had been tricked: Laban had given him Rachel's sister, Leah. The deception was possible because the custom was to bring the bride heavily veiled, and in the dark, to the groom after the feast. When Jacob confronted Laban with his fraud, Laban offered a compromise: If Jacob would just complete the seven days of the marriage festivity for Leah, at the end of the week Rachel would be his also. But there was an added hitch: Jacob would have to work *another* seven years for Rachel's bride money.

UNDERSTANDING RACHEL'S CULTURE

To understand Rachel we need to understand the cultural context in which she lived, as well as the cultural factors that shaped her and her family. Rachel lived in a patriarchal society in which power was held by the father and distributed, when it was distributed, to other men. Men held powerful positions, and men's voices were heard over women's. Rachel's culture was also polygamous. She and her sister and their handmaidens lived in an intricate system of multiple wives who often competed for status in the household. Rachel also lived in a society where it was customary to worship idols. These idols often existed in the form of household gods or statues that were believed to embody their deities and were thought to provide protection and bring prosperity to the household. Consequently, owning these idols brought additional status and authority to the household patriarch.

The primary economy of this country was shepherding, so it is especially significant that, in this male society of shepherds, Rachel was called a shepherdess. She was, indeed, a leading lady who, probably in the absence of older brothers, had learned her father's trade. Unfortunately, Rachel also lived in a society in which women did not usually inherit any of their father's wealth. So Rachel and other women had to depend on others—their husbands or fathers—to survive.

All of these factors shaped Rachel: the family structure, the marriage customs, the worship system, the economic system. They shaped her sense of identity, the choices she made, and the way she interacted with others. Like Rachel, we, too, are shaped by forces around us. None of us are isolated selves. Family or kinship systems, our culture, our religious or spiritual traditions, the economic system of our society, our government, and the media collide and collude in constructing our image of ourselves. They collude in writing a script, and then persuade, tease, and sometimes coerce us to follow.

Each of us must decide how we will live our lives. But before we can begin to make that choice, we have to understand the factors that shape who we are. If we allow ourselves to be totally defined by external factors, we end up living according to the rules of the socially-constructed self rather than the principles of the God-created self. The expectations of others block us from doing the things we desire and achieving the dreams in our hearts. We end up living the life of the "other woman"—the one cheating us out of being real with ourselves and others. Instead of expressing our creation in God's image, we feel obligated to fulfill society's image. At times we may feel crushed beneath the weight of expectations, shoulds, and oughts heaped upon our backs.

How we see ourselves affects how we interact with, relate to, and communicate with others. Look at Rachel and Leah again. Each sister saw herself the way others saw her. Each sister valued what others valued in her. Rachel was valued for her looks; Leah was valued for her ability to bear children. Knowing that she was "second choice," Leah probably placed her hope for worth in her fertility. With the naming of each son, Leah voiced her inner yearning: When she named Reuben, she cried, "Surely my husband will love me now"; with Simeon, she lamented, "The Lord heard that I was not loved"; with Levi she hoped, "Now at last my husband will become attached to me"; and with Judah's birth, she proclaimed, "This time I will praise the Lord" (Genesis 29:31-35 NIV). Perhaps at last she began to shift her attention from Jacob.

While fertility was Leah's gift, it also created problems for Rachel, who remained barren. In a culture that defined womanhood by a woman's ability to bear sons, Rachel's inability to bear children probably left her feeling devalued and of little worth. Envious of her sister, Rachel demanded of Jacob, "Give me children, or I'll die!" (Genesis 30:1 NIV).

We can certainly identify with the longings of both sisters. When our sense of worth is tied up in external things we can't control, we feel inferior or worthless. When our sense of self is diminished, we, too, can become envious and demanding—even demanding that people give us something not in their power to give.

As human as the rest of us, Rachel concocted a plan: She decided to enlist her handmaiden to bear children for her, a practice common in that culture. Rachel's handmaid, Bilhah, started having children with Jacob on Rachel's behalf. As with Leah's sons, the names Rachel chose for Bilhah's children speak volumes: with the naming of Dan, she exclaimed, "God has vindicated me;" and with Naphtali, she boasted, "I have had a great struggle with my sister, and I have won" (Genesis 30:6, 8 NIV). It appears that Rachel was keeping score; her life had become a rivalry with her sister for significance.

I wonder, though, how Rachel kept score. If the measure was the number of sons, the scorecard would have read Leah—4, Rachel—2. I suppose Rachel might have rationalized her score based on her perception of Jacob's love for her, and her alone. I'm not sure about Rachel's thinking, but I know many women today who rationalize and distort reality to make themselves feel good, successful. When our sense of value is tied up in someone else—or something else—we can rationalize with the best of them, deceive ourselves about the worst of things, or sell ourselves short to maintain even the tiniest semblance of worth. Messed-up belief systems or thinking patterns distort how we see and value things every time.

For Rachel, everything changed when God "opened her womb" (Genesis 30:22 NIV). She gave birth to her first child, Joseph. After years of bearing the shame of barrenness, she finally bore a son. But apparently that wasn't enough to ensure her worth, for she exclaimed, "May the Lord add to me another son" (Genesis 30:24 NIV). No sooner had she been blessed with her first child than her inner longing for more surfaced.

This lesson is as timely today as it was then: As long as our sense of worth and value is dependent on some external thing, we will never be satisfied. We will always be looking for external measures of our worth. Our house won't be big enough. Our car won't be fast enough or new enough. Our partner won't be prestigious enough. Our significant other won't be cute enough, nice enough. Our boss won't be fair enough. When our sense of self is tied up in outward things, the issue will not be with *them*, but with *us* and how we see ourselves.

GRABBING FOR ALL IT'S WORTH

After Rachel's son, Joseph, was born, Jacob decided it was time to return to his own country. He asked Laban to let him go, along with his families—by now a large clan indeed. But as happens in many families around the issue of money and possessions, a debate ensued about how much Jacob was owed. According to the ancient custom, a portion of Jacob's bride's money was to have been set aside by Laban for Rachel and Leah. In addition, there were some promised sheep and goats. But things got sticky when Laban hid the animals, and Laban's sons started accusing Jacob of taking the family wealth.

Jacob had had enough! He sent for Rachel and Leah and exposed their father's deception and unethical practices. According to Jacob, Laban had changed Jacob's wages ten times, always trying to find ways to cheat Jacob. Rachel and Leah were angry with their father, for in cheating Jacob, Laban had also cheated them. Not only were they being excluded from their family's inheritance, but they were also denied their share of the bride's money for which Jacob had worked fourteen years. As they expressed it, "Is there still any portion or inheritance for us in our father's house? Are we not considered strangers by him? For he has sold us, and also completely consumed our money" (Genesis 31:14, 15 NKJV).

They were justifiably angry!

We can relate to their anger, for we too get angry when we are wronged. We get angry when we come to realize the damage that is done to our self-esteem and self-respect in a society that devalues womanhood. We should get angry when we see music videos that depict women as sexual objects. We should get angry when women's body parts are used to sell objects, such as cars and liquor. We should get angry when we hear that the average woman still earns only seventy-five cents for every dollar the average man earns. We should get angry when we bump our heads against the glass ceiling. We should get angry when we have to work in an environment decorated with posters of scantly clad women. We should get angry when we are not given the same opportunities for advancement or client contact as the men in our offices. We should get angry when we remember the abuse that we have suffered at the hands of cruel oppressors who claimed they loved us.

And anger is a great motivator for action!

Rachel's sense of worth had already been tattered by the daily wear and tear of competing with her sister for prominence. Now this revelation of her father's deceitfulness shredded her dignity one too many times. She took action: She stole her father's idols and hid them away for herself. In stealing her father's household gods, Rachel transferred the protection, prosperity, and value believed to reside in them into her own household.

I often muse and imagine Rachel grabbing one of those statues to hurl at her father. How many of us have wanted to throw something, anything, when we have been violated, cheated, hurt. Instead, too many of us passively react, turning in on ourselves. Depression, ulcers, and anxiety attacks are the body's emotional responses to our inability to express our anger adequately.

Maybe Rachel grabbed the idols to get back at her father for withholding from her and her sister their portion of the bride's money. How many of us want revenge when we are violated? "Lord," we moan, "expose him for what he has done." Our laments for revenge are really our hurting hearts crying out for justice: "Make it right, Lord."

Maybe Rachel just grabbed the idols to make sure she got hers. How many of us reach up, out, or over to get what we feel is rightfully ours? But in the process of stealing the "idols," we hurt ourselves more. We reduce ourselves to the level of the one who violated us.

Today our "idols" are those things we grab for that we hope will increase our value; they are the things we reach for outside of our relationship with our Creator. Our idols may be the things we buy to make us feel good about ourselves. Our idols may be the crowd we hang with in hopes of gaining popularity and acceptance. Our idols may be the substances we ingest to soothe our damaged emotions. Our idols may be other people whom we depend upon for validation or to prop us up. Sometimes our idols are the very positions of leadership for which we clamor and to which we aspire.

The problem is that stealing—or throwing or hoarding—idols doesn't help in the long run. We only end up exchanging one false value for another. Now don't get me wrong: I admire Rachel for asserting some type of agency or power to determine her own actions, given that for so long her actions were often dictated by others. How many of us likewise grab for something of worth? But in reality, to be the powerful transformative leaders we are called to be, we have to find our worth inside, not by grabbing any more external things.

RACHEL'S CHALLENGE

The high drama of Laban's cheating, Jacob's confronting, and Rachel's stealing made way for a new destiny. Jacob finally fled Laban's land and returned to his homeland of Canaan, but God wasn't done with them yet. God commanded them to pack up and make a pilgrimage to Bethel to make an altar before God. This trip called for some unusual preparation: Rachel and the rest of Jacob's clan were called to put away their idols. We too face this call before we can come to the place of our destiny. We too are challenged to put away our idols. We have a choice: We can hold on to our habits of comparing and competing and projecting a false image, or we can identify and discard anything and everything that has become a substitute for God.

The long and short of it is that Rachel chose to give up her idols. Although the Scripture account sums it up in just one verse (Genesis 35:4), giving up our idols can be a daunting task. When we surrender our idols, we come face-to-face with our own selves. When we put away our idols, trappings, and substitutes, we are left with us. But therein lies the potential: When we give up our idols, they give up their addictive hold on us. When we give up our idols, we can reclaim our true selves. We have the chance to discover, buried beneath the glitz and the façade, a valuable inner reserve that has awesome potential.

Rachel was challenged to just such a discovery, and so are we. In fact, the crux of being an effective leader depends on knowing and valuing our true selves and in having a strong internal sense of self connected to a real relationship with God our Creator. Leading from a false sense of self is perhaps the ultimate form of idolatry. The best leader is one who can be herself despite the pressures to compete, compare, and keep up.

Rachel and the rest of Jacob's clan were also invited to change their garments, to eliminate any coverings that spoke of their old identification. We, too, have the power to remove the cloak of cultural and societal myths that identify who we are as women. We have the power to dispel these stereotypes about what we can and cannot do, and allow our true identity to be revealed. Each of us can reclaim the powerful, beautiful, spiritual woman who waits to be released from the bondage of lies and myths.

The most effective leader is the woman who is able to separate herself from the expectations of her culture and value herself for who she is. She can separate fact from fiction—the fact of her inner self from the fiction of how others want her to be. The leader who discards her idols can embrace her calling, her destiny, and not be distracted by false gods and false values. She can then lead her organization, team, business, or ministry from a solid place of integrity and strength.

The Scripture text doesn't tell us what the journey to Bethel was like for Rachel, but we do know that Bethel was a significant place. Bethel means the "house of God" and was the place where Jacob had met God at the beginning of his journey eastward (Genesis 28:17-22). Now God was preparing Rachel and her clan for another meeting, an encounter with the true and living God, an experience that could not be replicated with household idols from her culture. Rachel and the rest of Jacob's clan were about to make a profound spiritual and cultural discovery.

For us, Bethel represents our God-place: the place in which we experience the presence of God, where we can listen to the voice of God, and where we can experience the love of God. This is a place to which our spirit is drawn in order to reconnect with the God who heals and restores us. Bethel is a place of transformation. In this place we can relinquish the false self that was constructed by society and forced on us from social stereotypes. In this place our dreams come alive and we can express the creativity that flows in us from the Creator. In this place we come to recognize our true voice in the reverberating echo of God's word. In this place we can come to accept the gift within us that is *us*.

COMING TO BETHEL

My friend Rae was diagnosed as HIV-positive at age twenty-four and with full-blown AIDS by thirty. She has been living with this disease for most of her adult life. As a person who used to define herself by her designer wardrobe, high-priced trinkets, high-profile dating list, and high-powered career, refusing to let AIDS define her was a significant challenge.

Abandoned by her birth mother, Rae had been raised in an abusive home by a stern woman she came to call Mama. Rae's Mama locked her out of the house at seventeen and, as Rae put it, "I've been steppin' ever since." This independent, well-educated woman described herself as "the quintessential Buppie"—young, professional, attractive, smart . . . drug and alcohol-free all her life. She stressed that she never had a one-night stand and was not promiscuous—the traits society often links to people living with AIDS—yet she contracted this disease that was to change the course of her life. So if anyone had a right to be angry with the disease that ravages like a murderous intruder, Rae did. She sometimes wore her anger as part of her Superwoman persona that she donned to survive a cruel world, as well as to fight the disease.

I got to know Rae when we were in seminary together. She let me see beyond the anger to the bright, compassionate woman of faith she had become. Down through the years, the anger, on top of the isolation and loneliness and physical and emotional pain, had worn her down, bringing Rae to her own Bethel experience. As she describes in her book, *Amazing Grace: Letters along My Journey*, "My anger at God was profound, and I questioned Him often. Superwoman was exhausted. Living with AIDS was too complex. Yes, I was tired, but my spirit wanted to go on. I understood that the person I used to be was gone. The new person had AIDS."[1]

At that point of emotional and physical exhaustion, Rae needed to find a way to live in peace with her disease. Her crisis led her to Bethel, and as she recounts it, "I surrendered to God. I just let go."[2] At Bethel, Rae found answers and the courage to bury her superwoman idol. At Bethel, Rae found the faith to ask God to use her to help someone else. With God's help, Rae turned her anger into activism and now leads a nonprofit organization dedicated to HIV/AIDS education and prevention. Annually, she speaks to thousands of high school students, churches, and community organizations, particularly the African American community, to bring people out of denial about this disease.

Rae uses her life to help bolster the self-esteem of women, to teach women self-love, and to help empower women to make better choices about their bodies and sexual lives. "At the end of the day, every woman must ask themselves, how much of me am I willing to sacrifice for a man? And every Christian Woman must ask herself, am I really living whole as God intended?"[3] In leading this ministry, Rae invites other women to take the journey to Bethel and remain in a safe and healthy place.

In the end, Rachel and the rest of Jacob's clan were invited to "dwell" at Bethel (Genesis 35:1 NKJV). We too are invited to become permanent dwellers in the divine places of our being. We can no longer afford to be visitors or sojourners in our own souls, visiting briefly in between times of being what others want us to be. We need to settle in and make ourselves at home in our own temple. Our bodies need to be places dedicated for worship and service, healing, and wholeness; places in which we express the divine image within us; places from which we release the divine power within us.

LEADING LESSONS

- The true value of leaders resides within. Leaders discover their God-given value.
- Leaders who grab power, position, and possessions often have their hands full but have empty hearts.
- The best leaders are the ones who can be themselves despite the pressures to compete, compare, and keep up.
- The most effective leaders are the ones who are able to separate themselves from the false expectations of their culture and value themselves for who they really are.
- Unresolved anger blocks the heart of leaders and affects leadership choices. Leaders channel anger into activism.

- Leaders who will truly transform lives must journey to Bethel.

REFLECTION AND DISCUSSION QUESTIONS

1. What idols have you held on to or have held onto you?
2. In what ways do these idols surface in your life? In your leadership?
3. In what ways have unresolved anger stifled your leadership potential? Take a moment to imagine what the possibilities would be if you could channel that anger into activism.
4. What's the first step you need to take on your journey to Bethel?

LESSON 5

RECOVERING THE QUEEN WITHIN:
Insights from Esther
on Leadership Formation

Study Text: Esther 2:1-18, 4:1-17, 5:1-3, 8:3-8

The Persian culture in which Esther lived valorized the compliant woman, and Esther, like many young women of the empire, was raised to conform to that ideal. Yet ultimately Esther transformed the system that tried to destroy her people. Through a series of transitions, she uncovered her leadership potential and developed her leadership identity. As she navigated each transition, a new Esther emerged, until the leader that was buried deep inside of her came forth.

༺༄༻

I was in Seattle preparing to teach on "Esther the Intercessor" from my book *Leading Ladies*. As I was in prayer, the Holy Spirit whispered into my heart, "You can't really appreciate the Queen that Esther became until you come to understand the process of recovery she went through." From this insight, I came to see leadership development for women as a type of recovery process of the God-endowed but *buried* leadership gifts within us. Our Creator has gifted us with leadership potential, but often our leadership gifts remain hidden, unexposed, dormant and un- or underdeveloped, unless we consciously access and cultivate them. Leadership formation—forming leadership identity, uncovering leadership potential, and developing leadership skills—is affected by our culture's understanding and reinforcement of gender ideals and expectations.

I was drawn to the second chapter of the book of Esther. I had spent so much time on the fourth chapter, where she was called "to the kingdom for such a time as this" (Esther 4:14 NKJV) that I had missed a very important dimension of Esther's life: She had experienced and overcome great loss at several junctures in her life. Yet each of these junctures served as a developmental place in which this young woman grew and ultimately emerged as Queen.

At the heart of Esther's story is the making and forming of the Queen. Esther's journey to the throne room consisted of a series of smaller treks that can be described by four formative places in her journey: Mordecai's House, the Women's Quarters, the King's House, and the Throne Room. These places are akin to the "holding environments," which Robert Kegan in *The Evolving Self* describes as the psychosocial contexts "in which and out of which a person grows" to maturity.[1] Esther's growth to maturity was also her growth to leadership.

We need to grasp each of these places in the journey not only to understand Esther's growth and development, but our own as well. The places of Esther's leadership journey can help us reflect on and make sense of our leadership path. Esther provides a model for our growth, development, and spiritual empowerment as leaders.

MORDECAI'S HOUSE

According to the story, Esther had lost her father and mother, apparently at a young age.

Losing a parent at any age is potentially devastating because it means the loss of an opportunity to relate to and be nurtured by a loving mother and father. The Bible does not tell us much about Esther's reaction to her parents' deaths. We are told only that an older cousin, Mordecai, a Jew of the tribe of Benjamin, took her in and raised her.

Thank God for the Mordecais who help us through our periods of grief and trauma! Just as Mordecai's House would have been crucial to Esther's development and formation, we too have our Mordecai's Houses where we are nurtured, protected, and shaped. Our Mordecai's House represents a place of safety, healing, protection, and religious training.

Mordecai's House is a place where the foundation is laid, where our core identity is formed, and our values are shaped. For some, this foundational place is the home of their family of origin, or as it was for Esther, the home of adoptive or foster families.

For others, this place of safety, this experience of being protected, does not happen until years later, after some trauma. For women who have survived abuse, a women's shelter may become their Mordecai's House.

Mordecai's House is also a place where we are shaped by the expectations of our family and friends. Carol Lakey Hess, in her book *Caretakers of Our Common House: Women's Development in Communities of Faith*, describes this phase of human development as marking "a person's capacity to listen to and comply with the expectation of his or her group. These abilities prepare the way for later interdependence."[2] Our time in Mordecai's House is crucial, for it is in this place that our capacities for developing healthy interpersonal relationships, which are core to future leadership, are formed. It is also in Mordecai's House that we need to nurture young girls to become confident and assured, and to help them develop the skills necessary for forming relationships, reaching goals, facing conflict, and accepting their emerging strengths and power.

A few years ago, I was back in my hometown visiting my family, and my niece Kristen joined me on my daily power walk. At ten years old she was already five-feet-two-inches. As we walked, I noticed that Kristen's long legs kept her a few paces ahead of me. I tried to catch up with her, but couldn't. Finally it dawned on me that she was intentionally outpacing me. When we finished our walk, we plopped on the living room floor of my mother's home to stretch and take off our walking shoes. Kristen looked up smiling from ear to ear and said, "Grandma, I went walking with Aunt Jeanne and out walked her!"

Surprised by her remarks, I said, "Kristen, strong women don't have to brag about their accomplishments!" She looked down and focused on her shoes. Her smile had vanished.

Later I was stung by my reactions to Kristen's remarks. I went to her and said, "Kristen, you are really becoming such a wonderful young lady. You are smart and a good athlete. And I want you to be proud of what you can do. I never should have reprimanded you for bragging because what you were doing was not bragging. You were stating fact—you *did* out walk me, and that is something you can be proud of. I want you always to be comfortable with your accomplishments and be able to say what you can do with confidence! Please forgive me for making you feel badly about that."

How many of the women of my generation were told we were too womanish, or that we were getting a little beside ourselves, and were brought in line quickly—teaching us a false sense of humility that left us conflicted about our abilities? For some of us, those feelings of self-doubt linger to this day and bleed into our leadership. Yet sometimes, even the best of us fall into sending mixed messages to our young girls—perhaps the same limiting messages we received in our own early holding environments.

From Mordecai's House, Esther beckons to us to nurture our young girls and encourage them as they develop their sense of self, as they come to assume their emerging sense of power, and as they sort through their options. This place of safety lays the foundation for our future leaders.

In each of our lives, however, there comes a time when we have to leave Mordecai's House. We have to move from these safe havens, out of our comfort zone and on to the next place. Some of us leave Mordecai's House easily, some of us are let go from Mordecai's House too soon, and others of us stay so long we practically have to be kicked out. But there always comes a time to leave. So it was for Esther. The King of Persia placed a call for beautiful young maidens to be brought to the palace so that he might choose his new wife from among them.

THE WOMEN'S QUARTERS

So it was that Esther was taken to the King's palace and entrusted to Hegai, who had charge of the King's harem. The sense of the Hebrew language in this text suggests that perhaps Esther was taken against her will, that she did not volunteer to go the harem.

A harem literally means "sanctuary" and was usually a secluded house or part of a house allotted to women. Notwithstanding our Western stereotypical perception of the harem as a place of beautiful, sensual maidens, the harem was the place in polygamous cultures where all of the women—wives, concubines, female relatives, and servants—lived. Some versions of the Bible call this place the "women's quarters" (Esther 2:11 NKJV).

For Esther, this transition into a new stage of her life meant more loss. By being forced into the King's "beauty contest," she lost the comfort of her home environment. She may very well have lost her youth. She was a young girl thrown into a very grown-up situation. She even lost the privilege of revealing her true identity, since she was ordered by Mordecai to keep her Jewish heritage secret.

Yet in spite of the losses, Esther grew and gained favor. The Women's Quarters became a place of her preparation. For twelve months she and the other young women brought here were given special food and luxurious beauty treatments to prepare them for their visit with the King. For twelve months Esther lived under the tutelage of Hegai, the steward of the harem. She even gained some perks: extra beauty treatments, a special place in the harem, and seven maidservants. All the while Mordecai hovered nearby to see how she was doing.

From Esther we learn how critical the Women's Quarters are to the formation of the Queen. While our Women's Quarters aren't the ancient Persian harems of Esther's day, the concept represents a place where we as women are groomed for our future assignments. It is a place of preparation. It is a place where we learn our value as women. It is a place where we come to appreciate the full dimensions of ourselves—our ethnicity, our culture, and our relationship with God. It is a place where we learn the value of other women, where we learn to get along with and work with other women. It is a place where we learn to harmonize in the choir before we are given the lead solo. It is a place where we learn to work in ministry in order to understand the heart of women before we ascend to lead in ministry.

For some of us, that early preparation occurred in our mother's homes: listening around the kitchen table as our mother's and her friends talked and passed on wisdom and values to us. Or it occurred at our mother's "apron strings" as she cooked and baked, passing on family secrets about the recipes and the traditions of her family. For some of us, this place of female bonding occurred in sororities, as we learned the traditions of our sorority and bonded and banded with our sisters. For some of us, this place of women's preparation occurred in the church "missionary society." These church groups, comprised mostly of women, were the places where we learned to pray and worship, as well as make decisions, handle conflicts, and solve problems. Even though we might not have realized it at the time, these Women's Quarters—the places where we came to appreciate our gifts as a woman and learned to value other women as gifted creations of God—were vital in our formation.

I hail from strong matriarchs on both sides of my family. My maternal grandmother had six daughters, and my paternal grandmother had four. In all, I have twenty female first cousins, nine of whom lived within a five-mile radius of me at some point of my growing up years. Consequently, my Women's Quarters experience occurred early for me. I played and interacted with my cousins from the time I was a child, which helped me shape my sense of self as a young Black girl. We loved each other, trusted each other, looked out for each other, helped each other, got mad at each other, and made up with each other. My younger sister did not come along until I was almost ten years old, so it was from my first cousins that I first learned the value of sisterhood. My experiences with my cousins helped me respect—and expect—healthy relationships with other women.

Yet as I grew up and entered into various workplaces or community and church environments, I soon realized that not all women had the affirming experience of the Women's Quarters that I had. And even among those who did, too many women succumb to the pressures of patriarchy: male-dominated systems designed to keep men in power. Too many of us believe that we have to compete with and put other women down in order to garner the attention of male power holders for promotion and recognition, all the while diminishing our true feminine power.

In some contexts women working against women has become legendary. Pat Heim and Susan Murphy, in their book *In the Company of Women*, identify strategies that women use to undermine other women: gossip, spreading rumors and divulging secrets, publicly making insinuating or insulting comments, undermining and sabotaging, and purposefully snubbing and withdrawing friendship. These strategies are *indirect,* rather than direct aggression. Heim and Murphy argue that women's early experiences with play teach us to collaborate rather than compete, to focus on process rather than goals, and to keep the power among us "dead even."[3] Yet, they also argue that girls' early experiences do not teach us how to handle conflict directly. "In fact," they write, "we've learned not to compete, not to speak up, not to draw attention to ourselves, and most definitely not to act too powerful or other girls won't like us and may even reject us."[4] Unfortunately, these too are the lessons drawn from the Women's Quarters that affect how women lead.

My sense is that we need to build new Women's Quarters where we can go for healing, for valuing of each other, and for learning direct ways of dealing with each other. For instance, we have numerous national women's conferences that attract thousands of women. Into these conferences or alongside of them, we could incorporate skill-building courses that teach women effective leadership skills, such as communication and conflict resolution. At the local church level, more and more of our women's ministries need to get away from just having an annual women's day service in which women dress up in the same color and invite a woman to speak to the congregation. Local women's ministries need to develop places for healing, such as support group and recovery ministries, and develop curricula that teach and reinforce life skills for women's success. And in our workplaces, we need processes and places by which women network, connect, and practice healthy leadership skills with one another. From the Women's Quarters, Esther beckons us to come for re-connecting, for preparation and pampering, and ultimately for grooming for greatness.

THE KING'S HOUSE

After twelve long months of preparation, the day finally came when the King made his choice: He selected Esther to become Queen. The King ordered a celebration and held a public festival in her honor. Esther had arrived at a place of prominence, but once again she faced a loss. In order to make the adjustment to the King's House, she had to let go of her harem-girl status. She had to make the transition in order to be Queen.

Sometimes we too make it to the King's House: We get that new job, receive that promotion, earn that degree, receive that special recognition or award. Yet along with our promotions, we have to grapple with loss and make adjustments for success. We have to lose our old sense of self and see ourselves in our new role. Some people sabotage their success because they never adequately let go of their former roles. Failing to let go of the past before moving on to the future is like the trapeze artist who fails to let go of the rung behind her, while striving to grab the rung in front of her. Trying to hold on to both rungs creates such tension that she will eventually lose her grip and catapult to the ground below.

Too many of us are falling because we fail to let go of old, worn out roles and expectations before we assume new roles. As we develop and grow and mature into authentic leaders, we cannot go back and pick up habits or patterns from our past that were not effective for us then. Each stage of our growth requires—and enables—us to let go of old things that did not work for us.

I once heard Star Jones Reynolds describe this letting go on the television show *The View.* She told a story about a first date with a young man. As he talked about one of his hobbies, Star commented to him, "That's interesting that you enjoy that, but I don't." She went on to tell the television audience, "The old Star would have tried to impress him and pretend that I liked that hobby." In her own way, Star was acknowledging her growth as a woman—a woman who had let go of her old way of doing things and who no longer had to impress by pretending.

Did Esther have to keep pretending? Yes . . . and no. She still had to keep the secret that she was Jewish, as she had promised Mordecai. Yet, as every leader must do, she had to differentiate between her old self and her new self. Her beauty may have landed her on the throne, but her use of her power would determine her future. The effectiveness of her choices and decisions would ultimately decide the fate of her people.

Esther was in a position to discover her potential, to fulfill who she was becoming. God's plan for Esther was far broader than just marrying the King. The King's House was an entrée for Esther, not the end in itself. Esther had to discover for herself why God had strategically placed and prepared her to fulfill kingdom purposes.

The true Queen arises when the needs of the kingdom come to the forefront. Too many of us get excited because we make it to the King's House but never ask *why* we are where we are and *what* we are supposed to do now that we are here! In other words, recognition alone is not enough for the true Queen. The true Queen is more than a trophy wife or an ornament to display. The true Queen is more than a token to fill a quota. The true Queen has to realize she is where she is for a reason and has great things to offer. The true Queen comes to recognize she is where she is by divine appointment.

For some of us, the Queen inside is raring to get out. But for others of us, like Esther, it takes a crisis for the true Queen to surface, to rise to the occasion. Esther's true beauty as Queen didn't emerge until a crisis forced her to make some hard choices, to take some risks to walk in her God-given power and authority.

Crisis brings out the true Queen—the empowered Queen—not the beauty queen. Crisis shows us the caliber of the Queen within us. Many of us don't even know what is in us—but God does! There comes a point in our lives when we, as women, must choose to keep moving forward and accept God's plan for us, or to stay where we are, comfortable in the King's House. We must choose to put ourselves "out there" or choose to stay hidden—cute but concealed, gifted but not effective, talented but dormant. So it was with Esther: She chose to move forward.

THE THRONE ROOM

In reality, even though she was the Queen, Esther had only limited access to the King: She could only come when the King called (although I am sure she had to be ready to come at a moment's notice in case he did call!). The punishment for *anyone* going to the Throne Room without being called was death.

But there came a time when Esther had to make a decision to walk in the authority of her position into the Throne Room on her own. The crisis was precipitated when one of the King's top advisors, Haman, persuaded the King to sign a decree giving orders to annihilate all the Jews in the land. Esther's cousin Mordecai got word to her, with a desperate request that she go to the King and plead for her people. It is at this crux of the story that we hear the famous challenge: "Yet who knows whether you have come to the kingdom for such a time as this?" (Esther 4:14 NKJV).

The decision Esther faced was literally a matter of life or death. She risked death by seeking an audience with the King without being called, and she risked death by revealing her identity as a Jew. She had to break through her barrier of fear and claim her authority. Esther made the hard choice: She chose to petition for her people.

She prepared by praying and fasting for three days, and then she donned her royal robes and stood before the King in the Throne Room. But she did not stand alone. God stood with her, and the King received her. He granted her simple request that he and Haman come to a banquet she would prepare. As Esther had carefully planned, one banquet led to another, and to her final petition: "Let my life be given me . . . and the lives of my people—that is my request" (Esther 7:3 NRSV). It was in the Throne Room that the King gave Queen Esther the authority to counteract Haman's decree to kill the Jews.

Esther's courageous actions saved her people. Her decision to enter the Throne Room created the conditions in which the empowered Queen—the true Queen—could come forth. Her decision brought her to the place where she could begin to walk in her true Queenness.

The Throne Room was the place of Esther's destiny, the place to which she was called to change the kingdom. In this place she lost her sense of helplessness and accepted her identity as Queen. In this place she overcame her fear and embraced her power. In this place she remained clear on the issues and acted decisively. In this place she drew on all the resources available to her—her courage to go against the establishment, her God-given ability to devise a plan of action, and her belief in God's vision for her people. In this place she stepped into freedom to choose her own life, rather than wait to be chosen. In this place she became the Queen she truly was.

The Throne Room is a place of power, a place from which power flows and things get done. The Throne Room is a place of destiny, a place to which we are called. The Throne Room is that place each of us comes to and recognizes *this* is where we are supposed to be. For many women, the Throne Room is a place of career culmination, a place to which we have ascended after jumping the appropriate hoops, playing the games, yet holding on and growing in our core sense of self. It is a place to which we ascend and revel in our inner strength, and we demonstrate courage by focusing our leadership on worthy causes, other people, and "giving back." The Throne Room is a place where we express our spirituality as an integral part of our leadership identity. The Throne Room is a place where the leader's true power is manifest.

Lana Thompson was probably one of the most gracious women I've known, and she wore her power like an elegant evening gown. I first met Lana when I did a morning radio segment on a Chicago-based radio station for which Lana was the National Sales Director. She stopped me in the hall one day to let me know how much she enjoyed my teaching. I also found out that we attended the same church, and I had not even known it. After that, whenever I would see her at church functions, or run into her in the hallway at the station, she had a way of calling me "sister" that evoked in me warm feelings of what it meant to be truly connected in the Christian family.

A few years after our first hallway meeting, we met at a pre-concert reception held at our church. In the course of our conversation, she let me know she had just been promoted to station manager. My eyes brightened and my smile widened as I congratulated her on this honor: She would now lead one of Chicago's largest urban format stations. She clearly was competent and a leader recognized for her influence and ability to get results.

Yet I sensed that, for Lana, this promotion was more about living out her purpose as a woman of faith than propping her ego with title and position. She confirmed this as she held my hands and said, "Pray for me." This powerful woman was at a stage of her career and leadership that she did not have to be overly concerned about other people's opinion of her. She had proven she could make the tough decisions and would continue to make those decisions. She had proven she could build strong teams and a successful, profitable organization. She had stood up to the challenges of leadership in a man's world and had not lost her femininity. She showed courage and toughness and remained gracious. Yet with career power, she never lost sight of the source of her true power: her faith in God who had brought her to this place of leadership "for such a time as this." She had reached a place in her life and leadership in which she actualized her goals while helping others to do likewise. We lost Lana to cancer just seven months after that conversation. The community's and nation's tribute to her was evidence of the widely held respect people had for her.

Too often we see the finished product of powerful women but are blind to the process that God used to make them who they have become. Esther's growth and ascension into her Queen-ness began with a series of smaller treks or steps. The transitions of her journey to power and empowerment provide us with a model for our journey to leadership. At each juncture we too need to let go of the old, take time to grieve what is lost, prepare for the new, and then walk forward into our purpose.

Too many of us fail to appreciate the powerful woman that is being formed inside of us. Too many of us never fully walk in our greatness. Too many of us fail to make the full impact that we could. There is a Queen inside of each of us—a gracious, influential yet powerful woman—waiting to ascend to greatness. That Queen is the leader within that is needed to change the world around us. That Queen is the woman of dignity and grace that is being positioned to do powerful things.

LEADING LESSONS

- Leadership development is a type of recovery process of the God-endowed but buried leadership gifts within.
- The making of leaders doesn't just start with formal training in leadership development programs. Life experiences help to form leaders for life.
- The places where leaders come to appreciate their gifts and learn to value themselves and others as gifted creations of God are vital to leadership formation.
- At each juncture in their growth, leaders will need to let go of the old, take time to grieve what is lost, prepare for the new, and then walk forward into purpose.
- If leaders are to continue to grow, times will come when they have to move out of their comfort zones and on to the next place of leadership.

REFLECTION AND DISCUSSION QUESTIONS

1. What was your Mordecai's House? How did you know when it was time to leave?
2. Where did you find your Woman's Quarters? How did other women help you prepare for your future?
3. List four words that describe the old you. What are some relationships, ideas, or habits associated with the old you that you now want to or need to let go of?
4. List four words that describe the new you that is emerging. What are potential new ways of interacting with people based on this new you?
5. Think of a specific transition you are making or have recently made. In what ways might the old you be blocking the Queen in you from emerging?

LESSON 6

STANDING BEFORE MOSES:
*Insights from the Daughters
of Zelophehad on Leading Change*

*Study Text: Numbers 26:1-2, 28-34;
27:1-11; 36:1-13*

We hail from a long line of women, such as Sojourner Truth, Elizabeth Cady Stanton, and Susan B. Anthony, who stood before power holders to lobby on behalf of women. They fought for equality, freedom, and justice. The Daughters of Zelophehad are five such women whose story speaks to us from the pages of Scripture about changing the status quo and leading change.

ৡৢৣ

A few years ago the leaders of a major denomination were struggling with the issue of women in their executive leadership ranks. Women clergy could be ordained as pastors but could not ascend to the next level of leadership, District Elder. At least in principle, that is. In practice, women in a few diocese or jurisdictions were assisting their Diocesan Bishops, performing the work of District Elder without the title. Now more women were calling for a shattering of the "stained-glass ceiling"[1] that prevented them from officially assuming key decision-making roles. In fact, a policy resolution to that effect had been initiated during the denomination's previous convention. Needless to say, the convention atmosphere the following year was highly charged as delegates awaited the pronouncement of the Board of Bishops that would decide the fate of women leaders. Much to the consternation of many, the Board recommended creating a new position of District Supervisor for women, giving women the rights held by male District Elders but not the same title. The Board was in essence creating a parallel leadership track for women, which was supposed to be equivalent to the men's role

Extensive discussion followed this motion, but only two women—in comparison to the dozen or so men who weighed in on the issue—were given permission to address the Bishops.

Even in deciding the lot of women, men dominated the debate! Yet these two women boldly represented the sentiments of a vast number of women of this denomination.

They passionately and clearly set forth their appeal. In essence, they argued: "This denomination has a grand history of supporting women in ministry, having ordained women into ministry from its inception nearly one hundred years ago. Yet other denominations have now surpassed us on this issue. Women comprise over seventy-five percent of our membership; limiting their executive leadership presence is a type of sacral apartheid. Elevating women into executive leadership ranks by giving them the responsibilities but not the title is the equivalent of creating a 'separate but equal' system—which in our history of racial segregation was dismantled by such court rulings as Brown vs. Board of Education. Separate is *not* equal."

In speaking up, these daughters of destiny embodied the courage and passion of five women in ancient Israel known as the Daughters of Zelophehad, who helped to shape the destiny of Israel. We do not often hear about the Daughters of Zelophehad, but they were important women in their community of faith.

LEADERSHIP IDENTITY

We first read about the Daughters of Zelophehad in Numbers 26 where they are included in the genealogy of the Israelites. God had commanded Moses to take a census of the nation because the first generation of Israelites who had come out of Egypt had died in the wilderness without reaching their destination, Canaan. God was preparing the new generation to enter into that Promised Land, and the Daughters of Zelophehad were part of this group, representing a new generation of leaders. Their significant place in the genealogy indicates their significance to the heritage of the community.

"Genealogy" is derived from the Greek word *genesis* and literally means "origin." But genealogies are more than listings of who begat whom, or who is whose son or daughter. Genealogies serve to remind us of the past and the key people who helped to shape a community or culture. Genealogies show us how certain people are connected to a culture and, in turn, how we are connected to them. Genealogies give insight into the core values of a culture, for it makes statements about who is included and who is excluded. Moreover, along with the listings of names often come stories about the people and why we memorialize them in our genealogies.

In Scripture a genealogy is an important tool for understanding leaders' beginnings. People named in the genealogy of a faith community were often considered the heroes and heroines of that community. For instance, Genesis 10:1-32 recounts the lineage of Noah and his sons. Genesis 11:27-31 provides the family lineage of Abraham. Matthew 1:1-17 recounts the genealogy of Jesus. So it is very significant that Numbers 26:28-34 and 27:1 record the names of the Daughters of Zelophehad and their connection to the community of faith.

Names provide important information about people, often yielding significant insight into their character, region of origin, or even destiny. Yet rarely are women's names included in the stories of the Bible. In fact, women's names represent between 5.5 percent and 8 percent of the total names given in the Bible. Of the thousands of people named in Scripture, distinct women's names total only one hundred sixty-two, the vast majority of which are in the Hebrew Bible.[2] Yet in Numbers, we are told that Mahlah, Noah, Hoglah, Milcah, and Tirzah were the daughters of Zelophehad. For all five sisters to be named speaks volumes about their importance in their community.

When we assume leadership roles, we likewise take on leadership names or titles. Titles suggest the significance of the leadership position to the organization or institution. Titles signify level and authority in the chain of command and organizational hierarchy. Titles do not suggest the *leader's* identity—that comes from within the leader—but titles do indicate *leadership* identity: the accepted expectations and responsibility that come with a leadership position.

At the convention where the denomination struggled with the issue of leadership identity, a great number of women knew implicitly that the title a leader has gives credence to his or her responsibility, role, and authority in the organization. In essence, these women were saying, "We want the responsibility . . . and the title that goes with it."

The early twentieth-century founders of this denomination cited the Apostle Paul's guidelines "to ordain elders in every city . . . if any be blameless, the husband of one wife, having faithful children, not accused of riot or unruly" (Titus 1:5-6 KJV) as reason for originally excluding women from the position of Elder. Paul's qualifications seemed to indicate that Elders were to be men, yet these early church leaders also supported women's call to ministry. They attempted to resolve this paradox by creating a type of "dual sex system"[3] in which ordained men were given the title Elder, and women in ministry were given the title Evangelist.

As times and perspectives changed, more of the leaders began to argue that New Testament women who served the church as overseers of local congregations—such as Priscilla, who led along with her husband, Aquila (see Lesson 8)—were the equivalent of Elders. They also argued that Paul gave instructions that male Elders be the husband of one wife because issues of divorce and marital fidelity were more prevalent among men in Greek cities such as Ephesus.[4] Still others pointed out that in Romans 16:7, Paul referenced a woman named Junia as being outstanding or notable among the apostles,[5] thus establishing the New Testament precedent for women's leadership at the highest levels of the church. Not a few of the delegates felt the issue was also about resistance to change, people wanting to preserve the status quo, to keep things "as they have always been."

CHALLENGING THE STATUS QUO

People in any system who resist change by protecting their interests are known as the "old guard." The old guard has nothing to do with the age of the leaders but with their mindset and their resolve to protect the old ways of doing things—in spite of mounting evidence for change. The old guard may fear that a new guard will automatically remove them from power.

The women who challenged the status quo of this particular denomination did not want to replace the old guard with a new guard of women who would weld and use power to hurt men. Their aim was to empower more women to live out and follow their leadership call. As these contemporary Daughters of Zelophehad spoke out, the Bishops and the entire congregation could not help but hear the underlying call for justice. The question became, would they listen?

When the ancient Daughters of Zelophehad raised their voices, the Israelite men listened. These ancient women leaders illustrate for us the importance of remaining aware of injustices, prayerfully building a case, enlisting the support of others, and courageously taking a case to the existing leadership. They provide a model for the process of challenging the status quo by speaking up on behalf of ourselves as women, and for other women.

The Israelite culture in which they lived was embedded with rules that excluded women. Just one example was the rule about who was—and who was not—permitted to inherit property. The inheritance laws dictated that only men could own property and, upon a man's death, his sons would inherit it. Inheritance was a critical, inalienable right that passed from father to sons. A man's name was continued not just in the genealogy, but also through land and property ownership.

The case of the Daughters of Zelophehad presented an interesting dilemma not quite covered by the existing laws and customs: What if a man died and left only daughters? Would his family name disappear from the rolls of land ownership? These were the important issues raised by the Daughters of Zelophehad on behalf of their father's name. Their father had died, and they were the only survivors—there were no sons. The question was what would happen to the family name and property.

The issue of women and inheritance was an important issue to this community. At the time of a woman's marriage, she was given a dowry from her family. This dowry became hers to take with her into her new family. The Daughters of Zelophehad stood to lose everything—including future marriage potential—if their father's inheritance did not pass on to them.

The process they used to raise the issue of inheritance for daughters is enlightening. First, Mahlah, Noah, Hoglah, Milcah, and Tirzah joined together to approach the existing all-male leadership. They operated in unity and spoke with one voice. Next the Daughters of Zelophehad provided a rhetorical argument that laid out the merits of their claim. They rehearsed who their father was, reminding the leaders that Zelophehad had done nothing worthy of having his inheritance stripped. They argued that his name should not be removed from his clan because he gave birth to daughters. Their position was that their father's property rightfully belonged to them.

The Daughters of Zelophehad could have remained silent and let the tradition of passing property on to sons continue. Yet in the name of their father they decided to speak out about injustice and try to change the existing state of affairs. They remind us of the importance of challenging the status quo by working *within the system* and appealing to the values that already exist within the community.

Many of us can envision a new state of affairs for our church, our community, or our places of work. Often the existing state of affairs, the status quo, prevents people from achieving their vision. In the denomination that struggled over women as Elders, a number of women were becoming so frustrated by the status quo that some were contemplating leaving. It is easier to maintain the status quo. It takes less creativity to keep things the same. It doesn't take a great deal of faith to do what you always have done.

But it takes faith and courage to speak up and find new ways to work together to bring about change.

Consequently women of this denomination began informally to rally together following in the footsteps of Mahlah, Noah, Hoglah, Milcah, and Tirzah. They held conversations among themselves. They prayed. Some researched, while others continued to speak up at their conventions. A few organized and participated in a forum to educate other members of the denomination on the issues of gender equality. Others wrote articles on women and leadership. In different ways, sometimes in loosely coupled ways, these church women "stood before Moses"—men in leadership who had the power to change the rules.

THE THEOLOGY OF GENDER JUSTICE

Moses was the leader of Zelophehad's community at the time, and he along with "the priest, the leaders, and the entire congregation" stood at the "entrance of the tent of meeting" to hear the Daughters' request (Numbers 27:2 NRSV). Can you imagine the courage it took for these women to stand before this daunting group? Fortunately, after listening to the Daughters' appeal, Moses "brought their case before the Lord" (Numbers 27:5 NRSV). Womanist theologian Delores Williams states that "when Moses takes the matter to God, the sisters' request becomes a theological issue."[6] Isn't the issue of women's leadership in today's communities of faith more than a sociological or civil rights issue? Isn't it also a theological issue? Claiming leadership is not a clamoring after title, as some have suggested, but rather a focused pursuit of a God-given calling that structural and organizational barriers must not limit.

Wise is the leader who takes the issues to God in prayer. Wise is the leader who is open to change, however it is initiated. When an autocratic leader tries to make decisions with no input from people, or no spiritual seeking, they in essence begin to play god. They reinforce a rigid system that protects their own interest and power as leaders. Spiritually sensitive leaders are open to change.

The Daughters of Zelophehad took a stance that flew in the face of all their tradition. They were willing to confront something they saw as unjust. They found the courage to challenge the existing laws of inheritance in a culture ridden with complicated rules that recognized only men. They stepped up and spoke out in front of the all-male leadership. They became catalysts for change not only for themselves, but on behalf of all women.

And God ruled in favor of the women. The Lord said to Moses, "What Zelophehad's daughters are saying is right. You must certainly give them property as an inheritance among their father's relatives and turn their father's inheritance over to them" (Numbers 27:7 NIV). God gave Moses a plan to take before the Israelites, a plan that was to change their inheritance laws and serve as a precedent for case law for generations to come. God moved Moses to rule on behalf of the women.

On that fateful day when the divided denomination voted, God moved the congregation to support the women. They voted to have the Board of Bishops figure out a way for women to be elevated to the higher offices and be given the same title as men. What the women of this denomination were saying was right. The Bishops were to report back the next year with a plan to equitably elevate women to the next level of leadership and forever shatter the artificial barrier that had prevented them from pursuing their God-ordained leadership potential.

And so it was, a year later, again after much debate, the rights of women prevailed. The delegates of the convention voted to grant to women the title District Elder, with all corresponding responsibilities, rights and privileges, and to give Diocesan Bishops the right to elevate women to that office at their discretion.

THE RIPPLE EFFECT OF CHANGE

Any change in a system ripples through the system and creates the potential for more change. After Moses changed Israel's inheritance laws, the tribal leaders of Manasseh foresaw a problem with the new ruling, and they proposed another change. They realized that if a woman owned her inheritance and then married into another Israelite tribe, the inheritance would go with them to the new tribe. They wanted Moses to do something to prevent this economic loss to their own tribe.

Just when the women were granted the rights of inheritance, marital custom in their patriarchal system created conflicts that might erode the very right for which the Daughters had advocated! Even with the Daughters of Zelophehad, one step forward seemed like two steps backward.

Even in the denomination where women won the right to serve as District Elders, their right to serve as Bishops is now being challenged. One Diocesan Bishop elevated a woman to the position of Suffragan Bishop (an auxiliary or assistant to the Diocesan Bishop), and his peers challenged him, stating it was not in their bylaws to make women Bishops. For some in this denomination, granting women the right to assume the office of Bishop is the next logical extension after making women District Elders. For others, if women are to be made Bishops, they must go through a process similar to that used to win the right to be District Elder. So the debate continues, and the leaders of this and other denominations continue to seek the mind and will of God to accommodate and make room for the gifts and callings of women in its highest ranks.

In ancient Israel, Moses also struggled with accommodating women's rights and ensuring stability in the community. The accommodation Moses made was to maintain that the daughters could own land, as long as they married within their tribe. This passage cannot be used to justify contemporary marital selection, but it does affirm the process and outcomes that ancient women took to ultimately secure their rights to inherit a piece of the Promised Land.

In fact, their actions alert women today of the necessity of properly preparing for the challenge that may come if the change is not properly implemented. Here are some things that we contemporary Daughters of Zelophehad need to consider as we continue to stand before Moses and work for change within our communities of faith.

✿

Build a network of change agents. Just as the Daughters of Zelophehad together approached the leadership of Israel, so must the women of churches, denominations, or religious institutions unite to raise a collective voice. Too often too many of us have tried to initiate change on our own. Instead, we need to build a network of change agents. Networks of like-minded women (and men) can provide spiritual and social support, resources, information, strategy, and access. Women auxiliary leaders, lay directors, pastors, and ministers need to come together in forums to keep the real issues on the table. We need to call upon more women scholars to continue to explicate the issues. We need to include women writers to disseminate our stories in various publishing outlets. We need to bring the woman in the pew into the discussion so she can share the ways in which she is excluded in various venues. We need to network with our national, state, and local women's associations for meeting, talking, supporting, affirming, and sharing successes and failures.

✿

Encourage the advocacy of Moses. Another necessary step is for more men to come forward to advocate on behalf of women's full inclusion at every level in the leadership of our churches and denominations. Just as Moses became an advocate for women among the other male leaders, most churches, denominations, and religious institutions have a number of powerful men who can serve as Moses for women. Some of these male leaders have been vociferously supportive of women in the debate, while others have stayed on the fence, refusing to speak one way or the other. Silence does not automatically mean consent. Women need to stay in dialogue with these men and affirm their support. We also need these "Moseses" to talk to other men, in ways that only men can initiate difficult conversations with each other, and enter into dialogue with them to explore their fears and concerns about change. These men can pave the way for women to hold more open dialogue with those who seem to resist change.

Develop systems of accountability. Churches, denominations, and other religious institutions need to be able to provide quantitative measures of the presence of female leadership within their ranks at all levels. Current leaders need to scrutinize their systems, policies, and practices to make sure they are creating an environment that allows women to respond to the call of God in the same way that men respond to the call of God. As more jurisdictional, diocesan, and regional leaders are required to provide reports that document the demographics of their leadership ranks, more leaders will come to see—through numbers—the staggering inequities that exist within the leadership ranks of our churches and denominations.

Develop formal systems of leadership formation and preparation. Even though more women are being educated in our seminaries and Bible colleges, women continue to be passed over for pastoral placements, and they struggle to plant and maintain church start-ups. Women continue to be overlooked for denominational and administrative appointments. The customs and practices of most of our churches and denominations show us that the line of leadership accession is as much political as it is spiritual. For its entire history, top leadership in most of our denominations has been passed down from men to other men. No doubt, there is an informal system of relationships, such as mentoring and coaching, that undergird such a system. Women have not only been excluded from the formal leadership structure, but they have also been excluded from the informal system that grooms men for top leadership. One remedy would be to develop a system in which the leadership potential of women is cultivated by assigning them mentors who could train and coach them on the "insider" dimensions of denominational leadership. Mentoring systems are often met by strong adverse reactions from the people who have previously held the positions of exclusive privilege, yet mentoring systems are necessary for formalizing the informal rules and creating a culture of equal access for women.

୧ଔ

Perhaps you see gender inequities in your church, denomination, or workplace. May the Daughters of Zelophehad's story encourage you *not* to look the other way. May these courageous women's voices resound within your heart to encourage you to step up and speak out. Only as more of us become agents of change and use our voices to call for the dismantling of unjust systems will transformation occur within the systems in which we worship and work. Only then will true transformation become a reality.

LEADING LESSONS

- Like leaves on a tree, sensitive leaders are stirred by the winds of change.
- Stepping up and speaking out is the first step to leading change.
- Leaders are change agents who uncover inequities and raise their voices for change.
- A team of leaders working for change must share a common vision and speak with a common voice.

- Leaders build and stay connected to their network of change agents.
- Leadership is not about replacing the old guard with a new guard. Leadership is not about guarding power but sharing and unleashing power.
- Leaders change the formal (and informal) processes to bring about lasting change.

REFLECTION AND DISCUSSION QUESTIONS

1. Tell something significant about one of the women in your family, church, or community "lineage." How did her actions help put something in motion for you and your generation? How does her story help to motivate you to work for change today?
2. Think of a time when the "practice" began to clash with "principle" in your place of work or worship. What happened? What changes resulted from this clash?
3. What issues of gender inequality do you see in need of being addressed in your congregation or community?
4. Who in the congregation or community might support you in challenging the status quo? Who might form a team to approach the existing leaders? What are the facts and merits of your case? How might you best present your case?
5. Examine your current network of leaders. Who makes up this network? In what ways might this network become a vehicle for establishing unity and collective voice on behalf of gender equality?

LESSON 7

PAVING THE WAY FOR MINISTRY:
Lessons from Lydia
on Pioneering Leadership

Study Text: Acts 16:6-15, 40

Down through the ages women have played a critical role in paving the course for the birth and the continued growth of the church. Sometimes women have served in formal or official leadership roles, and at other times they served in informal leadership roles. In either case, women have helped to shape and influence the church. One such person was the New Testament woman Lydia. Even though Scripture devotes only four verses to her, she is a pioneer of the Christian faith: She is credited with being the first recorded Christian convert in Europe. She donned many leadership roles that encourage us in our multiple leadership roles.

☙❦☙

I had arrived the day before my big presentation. The next day was critically important, and I wanted to have plenty of time to get settled and be mentally prepared for it. One of my clients was launching a new initiative for executive women, and they wanted me to be the trainer to facilitate their in-house women's leadership sessions. I had completed the first phase of my certification training and now was scheduled to facilitate my first session under the watchful eye of Kayla,[1] my master trainer. If it was successful, I would receive my certification as master trainer—which not only meant a possibility of additional business but also the opportunity to bring my passion for empowering women for leadership and service into the corporate world.

After checking out the session room and making sure the participants' materials had arrived, I sat down in my hotel room to review my notes. I opened my laptop case to get out my materials—but they weren't there! After a few moments of checking every compartment in the case, then my suitcase, and even my purse, it dawned on me—I had left the folder with my notes and the facilitator's guide at home. I couldn't believe it; my heart sunk. As I plopped into a chair, my mind shouted, "What are you going to do now?"

After a minute or so, I jumped into action and called two women in my prayer circle back in Chicago. We had prayed each other through heartache and successes, and they knew I was in Dallas to run a program that could have a major impact on my work. I announced to each: "I am in a serious struggle here. I left the materials for the session at home, and I need you to intercede and cover me in prayer." Each agreed to pray; one prayer partner even started praying right there on the phone, asking God to give me wisdom and insight to handle this situation.

My next step was to leave a message for Kayla. I thought she might at least have a copy of the facilitator's guide, and that, combined with the Power Point presentation and video I had brought, might get me through. She came to my room as soon as she arrived at the hotel, and her first words—after telling me that she hadn't brought a facilitator's guide—were reassuring: "Let me allay your fears. You know this material inside and out. You have years of experience and formal training. Please don't get hung up on not having the facilitator's guide! You do have the video, don't you?" I pointed to the case as we both chuckled, elated that I had at least remembered to bring the video.

Before I went to bed that night, I prayed and placed the whole thing in God's hands. If this business were meant for me, it would happen. I awakened early the day of the training and prayed again. I arrived at the session room, carting laptop, video case, and freshly printed notes from the business center, where Kayla again reassured me that things would work out fine.

After receiving equipment instructions from the hotel's audio video technician, I went to pull my video out of its fancy case—and there was no video! I gasped. Then it occurred to me: In my diligence to review the tape one final time in my office, I must have left it in the VCR in Chicago! I was sunk. I found Kayla and sheepishly told her what I had just discovered.

Kayla placed her hand on mine and said, "We'll get through this! First of all, you know this stuff. The video is a good addition to the program [actually it was a highlight of the program], but you could teach the same points and lead an interactive discussion." I knew in my heart I could do that, and we began to do what many experienced trainers learn early in their careers: "design on the fly." I prepared to start the class, and Kayla went to call her East Coast company to see if there was even a remote possibility of getting another video delivered by lunch time.

Fifteen minutes before the session was to begin, the executive who had recommended me for this program, which was her corporate baby, stopped me. Before I could tell her what was going on, she asked me a question that was to change the course of my thinking about this day, and the entire program. Her timing proved to be a strategic reminder to me that God had "ordered my footsteps" and could handle my missteps.

"Jeanne, I've been meaning to ask you something. You're a Christian, aren't you?"

I looked at her in amazement and said, "Why, yes, I am."

She moved closer as if she were about to reveal a girlhood secret. "I thought so! I know we have placed a high expectation on you to get ready for this new program, and we have a lot riding on its success. I just wanted you to know that I've been praying for you."

The very woman whom I was so afraid of disappointing, because of her rank and title, was praying for my success! And God had her praying for me before I even knew that I would need her prayers so desperately. That conversation vividly illustrated for me that God places "Lydias" in even the most unlikely places. And like Lydia, a host of business women the world over intimately know the power of prayer as a strategic tool in their work lives, as well as in their worship lives.

I then let her know what was going on and asked her to continue to pray. You can only imagine how I felt as I opened the session for these executive women. I was nervous that I did not have my familiar trainer's trappings and had to make do with newly gener-ated notes, yet I felt a peace that so much prayer was going forth.

So I started, drawing on my years of teaching gender and communication in university courses and on the notes I did have, improvising as I went and trusting God for the outcome. Then, just as we were about to come back from the mid-morning break, good news arrived: Although Kayla's company could not get a copy of the tape to us in time, the distributor of the tape had located a Dallas-based customer who was willing to let us use their tape. Our prayers were answered: This customer was couri-ering the tape over to us!

Sure enough, the tape arrived just in time, and the participants were none the wiser. But I was the more awestruck by God's favor and influence of people and processes. I was the more apprecia-tive for a band of praying and faithful women who covered me in prayer. And I was the more humbled that even with all the stress before and during this session, the feedback at the end of the ses-sion was stellar. The client was more than satisfied, the observer was gracious, and I was certified.

Yes, this band of praying women—and I—believe that there is no arena of our lives in which God does not have power to inter-vene. Lydia must have believed the same thing, for she, too, was a member of a band of women who met regularly for worship and prayer and ultimately paved the way for a new ministry.

A FIRST-CENTURY PRAYING WOMAN
Even though we first meet Lydia at a riverside prayer meeting, her story really starts with the story of the Apostle Paul and his ministry teams. As some of the earliest missionaries, they traveled throughout the region, spreading the gospel of Christ, structur-ing churches, discipling new converts, and bearing witness to the Holy Spirit's presence in the world. Each time they arrived in a new city, Paul's custom was to find a house of worship or an infor-mal place of prayer where he could present the gospel.

On one such mission, Paul journeyed to Philippi, a major city of the region known as Macedonia. Apparently Philippi had no synagogue, so Paul and his company ventured to the outskirts of town in search of a prayer meeting. There they found a group of women who had gathered to pray. In the absence of a formal place of worship, these praying women were a testament to faith and faithfulness. Their faith in God ignited their desire to worship, and they took initiative, carving out a place of their own.

Lydia, described as a "worshiper of God" (Acts 16:14 NIV), is mentioned as one of the women who listened to Paul's message. It is not clear from this passage whether Lydia was the formal worship leader, but the very fact that Lydia is recorded by name as a part of this group gives us some insight into her faith. We learn later that she ran a business and led a household, so it is worthwhile to note that this very busy woman took time to pray with other women. Spirituality was an important dimension in the life of this powerful woman.

Lydia teaches us that the woman leader must tend to and nurture her spiritual core through prayer and worship. Gathering together with other praying women is a powerful means of connecting with God and with each other. Throughout the centuries women have gathered to pray together. Even today, many churches in a variety of faith traditions host women's prayer groups that provide spiritual strength and support for women.

Scripture does not tell us about the things for which these women prayed, but it does give painstaking details to recount the journey of the Apostle Paul and his efforts to follow the leading of the Lord. Somehow, it seems, his journeying was related to their praying. While in the regions of Galatia and Phrygia, Paul and his company were "forbidden by the Holy Spirit to speak the word in Asia" (Acts 16:6 NRSV). Next they attempted to go into Bithynia, "but the Spirit of Jesus did not allow them" (Acts 16:7 NRSV). It was during his visit to Troas that Paul had a vision convincing him it was God's will that they go to Macedonia. Following this vision, Paul and his missionary team finally arrived at Philippi and met this band of praying women. Could it be God answered these women's prayers by bringing Paul to Macedonia?

The significance of Paul's arrival in Philippi is revealed in Lydia's conversion. When she heard the gospel of Jesus Christ, Lydia made a decision to join the Christian community. As the first recorded Christian convert in Europe, this praying woman became a pioneering woman, paving the way for other prominent women to join the Christian community.

Lydia's story reminds us that prayer opens our hearts to be responsive to God and the things of God. Prayer is the process of communicating with God—both talking to and listening for God. Prayer flows from a relationship with God and enables the child of God to enter into the realm of the Spirit. There is an intricate, yet delicate, link or tie between the spiritual realm and the material realm of our daily lives. Our faith is the bridge between the two, and prayer is the vehicle that carries us across the bridge. Through prayer, we gain access to the spiritual realm and affect what happens there, which, in turn affects what is happening in our realm of home, family finances, job, and nation. Through prayer we participate in God's work in the world.

A MATRON OF MINISTRY

Having joined the new community of faith, Lydia went a step further: She made a generous offer to Paul and his colleagues, "Come and stay at my home" (Acts 16:15 NRSV). Her hospitality spoke not only to her generosity in giving food and shelter but also to a heart committed to the work of God's people. Lydia's offer also attested to her affluence. Her house had to have been large enough to accommodate at least three or four visitors: Paul, Silas, Timothy, and perhaps the narrator of the passage.

She is described as being persuasive, urging Paul to consider staying at her house while he continued to evangelize the area. Her offer went far beyond an invitation for a few nights' stay. The result was that her home served as a place where Paul and his ministry team met with (and mostly likely prayed with) other believers in Philippi (Acts 16:40). Her gift of hospitality provided space and resources for the burgeoning ministry.

The role of "patron" was not new to the Christian church; it may have been a holdover from the church's Jewish roots. In her book *Women Leaders and the Church*, Linda Belleville points out that "Jewish women [were] singled out for their roles as donors, heads of synagogues, elders, priestesses, and mothers of the synagogue. . . . Jewish women took an active financial interest in their synagogue." In fact, these women "of independent means" were "financially active" throughout various regions of the Roman Empire.[2] It is in these roles of "ministry matrons," as I prefer to call them, that women such as Lydia helped develop the New Testament church. *The Women's Bible Commentary* informs us that wealthy women who functioned in such roles "in the developing Christian communities were obviously of critical importance to the early Christian community. The church depended upon the economic largess of women, particularly widows."[3]

Giving support to the fledgling works of ministry, or to business development, is a crucial role in the building, maintenance, and expansion of the work and ministry. As a matron—a leader who supports ministry in becoming stable and successful—Lydia's role was critically important to the forming Christian communities. Her leadership challenges us to prayerfully consider ways in which we as contemporary women can provide leadership in the financial, administrative, and decision-making activities of the church. Not many of us may have Lydia's resources, but countless numbers of us can, and do, birth and nurture ministries, small businesses, and community organizations.

A PIONEERING WOMAN

Some scholars contend that Lydia's story is shared in Acts for specific theological purposes: to show women who were thriving in other religious movements that there was a place in Christianity for prominent women. Yet even in the telling of Lydia's conversion story, the writer of Acts gives us a small glimpse into the lives of first-century women. We are told that Lydia was a "dealer in purple cloth" (Acts 16:14 NRSV). Purple dye and fabric were precious commodities, luxury items used primarily for clothing for the rich and famous. As a seller of purple fabrics, Lydia ran a commercial enterprise that would have put her in contact with the elite.

Though women have more recently swelled the business ranks, women business leaders are not new. Lydia's story reminds us of the prevalence of independent women adept in commerce and trade even in the first century. Though specific tasks may have changed in twenty centuries, Lydia shows us that women had business acumen long before we were given credit for such competence.

Lydia was also a leader of her own household, which probably consisted of family members as well as household workers. Lydia's influence over them was such that they followed her lead in spiritual matters: When she was baptized, they were baptized along with her. Lydia paved the way for her household to hear and respond to the truth of the Gospel.

According to Valerie Abrahamsen in her entry in *Women in Scripture*,[4] Lydia was probably a widow. No husband is mentioned in the passage, and according to the demographic patterns of her day, it was unlikely that she was divorced. Like Lydia, many women today have leadership roles in a variety of household configurations. Some women play major leadership roles in more traditional families. Others lead in blended family households, in single-parent homes, in a variety of relationship arrangements, or as single adults living alone. Even though the traditional family structure is changing, women's influence in the home is pervasive.

What we see in Lydia's leadership is her pioneering spirit. She and the other women launched out to meet in prayer when the institutional structures of her faith recognized only men. Traditionally, a *minyan,* or quorum of ten adult men, was required for communal prayer.[5]

I believe it was this same pioneering attitude that helped Lydia be open to the good news shared by the Apostle Paul. Lydia accepted the message of the gospel and embraced the evangelists. She carved out space for them, translating her gifts of running a business and household into running a ministry. And in so doing, she launched the European headquarters for the Apostle Paul's missionary team. Her story helps us to recognize our leadership, especially when the society or systems around us fail to appropriately name as "leadership" the things we do for the kingdom of God.

Unfortunately, institutions are not always the most welcoming places for pioneering women. For instance, the Department of Labor's Bureau of Labor Statistics predicts labor force participation rates for women aged forty-five to sixty-four will continue to rise through 2025, while rates for men are expected to shrink. Yet similar studies show a growing number of mid-career women—typically forty to fifty-five years old—are jumping out of successful careers, including possible advancement, reporting weariness with corporate politics and the glass ceiling.[6]

I once reported these trends to a client group, and an attorney challenged me: "Those trends seem contradictory. How can labor force participation rates for women increase while they are at the same time jumping out of successful careers?" I shot back, "What these trends are saying is that women will continue to work . . . they just won't be working for you—or other corporate entities."

More and more of us will be pioneering: carving out careers, ministries, opportunities that enable us to live, thrive, and make a living on our own God-given terms. When I started my business, I knew I wanted to provide training and consulting services that could unlock people's minds and hearts. I saw my business as my ministry and my ministry as my business. Laurie Beth Jones, in her book *Jesus, Entrepreneur: Using Ancient Wisdom to Launch and Live Your Dreams,* calls us pioneering women (and men) "spiritreneurs"—people who "fully integrate their soul in a workplace enterprise," who "launch endeavors that reflect their highest gifts and beliefs but also benefit others while doing so."[7] In other words, these leaders carve out new categories of work and service. That's what Lydia did, and her story reminds us of the power of prayer in these pioneering endeavors.

LEADING LESSONS

- Praying leaders prevail.
- The best business leaders understand the relationship between worship and work.
- Faithful leaders are pioneers whose example others want to follow.
- Giving leaders grow. Growing leaders give.
- Pioneering leaders influence at home, as well as in public.

REFLECTION AND DISCUSSION QUESTIONS

1. What opportunities do you have to join together with other women to pray? In what ways do these (or might these) prayer opportunities enhance you as a leader?
2. Think of women who have served as pioneers for you. In what ways have they paved the way for your leadership?
3. In what ways are you paving the way for other women? Carving out new categories for work and service?
4. Which of Lydia's leadership lessons do you want to develop more in your life?

LESSON 8

WORKING TOGETHER:
*Insights from Priscilla and Aquila
on Partnering in Leadership*

Study Text: Acts 18:1-3, 18-19, 24-28

*The fast growing Christian movement of the first cen-
tury had the same needs that any new organization has:
development, instruction, expansion, and oversight. The
Book of Acts gives us insight into how the early church
leaders handled these leadership functions. One such
church leader was a woman named Priscilla, who along
with her husband, Aquila, worked with the Apostle Paul
to help to establish the ministry in Ephesus. These partners give us insight into some of the relational dynamics of leadership such as collaborating, networking, and
mentoring.*

♋

In my work as a consultant, I often partner with other leaders to
secure business, co-facilitate training sessions, and develop new
products. I have found that together, as partners, we can do more
than either one of us can do on our own. I remember once co-
facilitating a training session in which I partnered with a consultant
named Eric.[1] We had worked together before, but this time we did
not seem to be flowing together very well. I felt that he was taking
too long to get through his segment, allowing the group discussion to go on too long. At the break I confronted him: I was going
to have to cut out my segment in order to get the session back
on track. Eric countered that he thought I had a vested interest in
sticking to the schedule, while he was satisfied to cut something as
long as the learners were truly being challenged.

The underlying issue was a failure to collaborate. Collaboration is a compound word that has at its heart the notion of
co-laboring. First and foremost, co-laborers see each other as
equal. They work together as a team, not as individuals who happen to be in the same room. The key to a successful partnership

is a collaboration that is based on trust, healthy respect for each other's talents and skills, and clear communication.

Eric and I then did something that I have found to be at the crux of collaboration: We identified mutual goals for our work together. Mutual goals eliminate the tendency of co-leaders to focus on their own activity and ignore the activities of the other leader. We were both clear that one of our goals was to work together with mutual respect, in a way that optimized each of our abilities. We agreed to divvy up future segments in such a way that each of us could play to our strengths, while at the same time, enhance the learning experience of the participants. Having talked through our issues and defined our mutual goals, Eric and I went on to complete a workshop that was rewarding for the participants and for us, and we laid the foundation for our continued work together.

The New Testament gives us a brief but poignant snapshot of a unique couple named Priscilla and Aquila who likewise partnered to get work done. This husband-and-wife team of the first century exemplifies collaboration as a leadership strategy. Their story helps us appreciate the intricacies of leadership partners, while giving us insight into the varied roles of women in the New Testament church. Women and men in our century—whether husband and wife teams or co-leaders—need to collaborate and partner much the way Priscilla and Aquila did.

In each of the six times Priscilla and Aquila are mentioned, they are *always* mentioned as a pair. Sometimes Aquila's name is listed first (Acts 18:2, 26; 1 Corinthians 16:19) and at other times, Priscilla (Acts 18:18; Romans 16:3; 2 Timothy 4:19). Priscilla herself must have been quite prominent, because placing a woman's name first in a dyad was not customary in written documents of that time. Perhaps the ordering of their names in these passages speaks of her status. Whatever their individual status, the consistent coupling of their names in ministry attests to the fact that they were considered equal partners in their ministry.

When we first meet Priscilla and Aquila in the Book of Acts, they had just been expelled from Rome because all the Jews had been ordered to leave. Now living in Corinth, they were working together in their tent-making trade. Priscilla and Aquila would have needed multiple skills in various crafts to be successful in their business. I imagine one of them must have been good at negotiating for the price of raw materials. One of them must have been a good tent designer. One of them must have had sewing skills. One of them must have been a good marketer to sell the finished product. Working side-by-side in their shop, Priscilla and Aquila would have had many opportunities to hone their collaborative skills and respect what each other did well. Their collaborative efforts were clearly successful, for they are identified in Scripture by their trade of tent making.

Working together on defined tasks helps leaders hone their communication skills. Pooling unique skills toward common goals helps leaders see the value of each person's contribution to the whole. Working side-by-side helps leaders understand that more can be accomplished together than alone. Most tasks—whether at work, at home, or at church—can be accomplished best when people have a chance to offer their specific gifts and skills. An effective leader understands the value of collaborating.

PARTNERS IN MINISTRY

Effective leaders combine their gifts to accomplish great things in ministry.

During my early years in youth and young adult ministry, few women in my denomination were serving in the top institutional roles. The president of the ministry in which I served could have expected me to serve in a mere perfunctory capacity, but I was blessed to serve as vice-president for a ministry leader who considered me an equal partner. Together we created a leadership team that was to end up providing innovative ministry for youth and young adults for almost five years. We worked in tandem, each bringing and respecting our specific gifts to the collaboration.

Years later, this ministry leader shared with me an epiphany he had about me serving as vice-president. I was the first woman in the circles we were part of who held the same education and skill sets that he did—*and* who also aspired to the same offices he held. Up to that point, he had competed with, and served with, only male leaders as they rose together up the ministry ranks. I was the anomaly and, as he tells it, "I realized very early in our administration that you brought a phenomenal set of skills and energy with you to this position. You needed a role as vice president that would allow you to use all of your gifts."

This ministry leader was a true visionary for innovative ministry, and I provided continuity between conferences and gave oversight to the daytime ministry activities. Working in tandem, each bringing and respecting our specific gifts, allowed us to collaborate in building life-changing ministry.

So it was with Aquila and Priscilla. When Paul arrived on the scene in Corinth, Priscilla and Aquila were already a team in their tent-making business, which they invited Paul to join. Together these three constructed tents—and built the church. Their joint enterprise may well have helped to underwrite the building of the Christian community. Since it was standard practice for members of the early Christian community to meet in houses, the people who hosted these house churches would have to have been financially secure enough to afford a house that would accommodate the burgeoning fellowship of believers. At the time of Paul's writing, Priscilla and Aquila were leading one such house church.

Just as in their collaboration in tent making, this team combined their specific gifts to collaborate in church building. One of them might have been good at contacting and inviting people to come. One of them might have been good at preparing the house, arranging furniture, making things ready for guests to arrive. One of them might have been skilled in leading worship. One of them might have been an excellent teacher of the gospel. However they combined their gifts, we know that worship, teaching, and fellowship occurred within these churches, and the ministry grew.

Priscilla and Aquila were so committed to the ministry that when the Apostle Paul left Corinth, they decided to accompany him to Ephesus to help establish a new church there. Eventually, Paul left them in charge of the church at Ephesus as he proceeded on to Jerusalem. The fact that Paul delegated authority to Priscilla and Aquila attested to their spiritual maturity and wisdom.

The Apostle Paul considered both Priscilla and Aquila to be fellow laborers with him in the gospel and was grateful for their contribution. We get some idea of the value Paul placed on this ministry team from some of his later Epistles. He sent greetings to them, acknowledging them as "fellow workers in Christ Jesus" and thanking them for risking their lives for him (Romans 16:3-4 NIV). He passed on their greetings to the church at Corinth: "Aquila and Priscilla greet you warmly in the Lord," along with "the church that meets in their house" (1 Corinthians 16:19 NIV). And in his second letter to Timothy, Paul specifically asked Timothy to greet them by name (2 Timothy 4:19).

Priscilla and Aquila clearly had what it took to co-lead, and they played significant ministry roles in the churches at Corinth and Ephesus. The two showed they could work effectively, and they provide us with a model of ministry partnership.

PARTNERS IN MENTORING

Effective leaders develop other leaders, who develop other leaders.

If you talk to any successful leader, he or she will tell you that they did not get where they are by themselves. God places other women and men in our path to help us understand the situations to which we are called, to help us hone our craft, and to give us support and guidance as we grow in our leadership.

In her book *Lanterns: A Memoir of Mentors*, Marian Wright Edelman, founder and president of the Children's Defense Fund, gives us insight into a wide array of mentors and mentoring systems. Edelman credits parents, community leaders, and teachers as being some of the first and most significant mentors in our lives. Edelman, however, also describes key people that took her under their wings at significant junctures of her journey. Her mentors, like all good mentors, established a relationship with her and provided feedback, insight, and support to her as she traveled life's journey.

Mentors were important in the development of the early Christian church as well. Gifted leaders were needed to shape the Christian communities of the New Testament. Yet who had the authority to speak? Who was to teach whom? How would new leaders be developed across such a widespread area? Who would ensure that the proclamations and teachings of the community were accurate? It would take many people working together to share the story of Christ and disseminate the significance of his life, death, and resurrection. It would take many passionate women and men sharing in mutual ministry to develop the church.

We are told the story of a gifted orator named Apollos whose teachings appealed to audiences and attracted followers. It turned out, however, that while he was "well versed in the scriptures" (Acts 18:24 NRSV), he had not been taught the full message. God placed Priscilla and Aquila in his life to teach him and equip him more fully to fulfill his destiny as a teacher of the gospel. Though the New Testament may not have labeled Priscilla and Aquila as mentors, the process they used to guide Apollos is instructive for all of us as leaders who would mentor someone else.

First, Priscilla and Aquila took the time to listen to Apollos' teaching for themselves. No doubt they had heard about the new charismatic orator who had come to town and was expounding the message of Christ. As they listened, they must have heard points that were inconsistent with the accepted teaching of the Church at that time. Leaders who mentor must listen to their protégés and discern their gifts, strengths, and weaknesses.

Secondly, Priscilla and Aquila "took him aside" (Acts 18:26 NRSV). In other words, they met privately with Apollos instead of confronting or challenging his views in public. Sensitive leaders respect the dignity of others and create a safe space in which to handle potential or real conflict. Leaders who mentor must make time for younger leaders to affirm their strengths, provide correction and direction, and help these fledgling leaders learn from their mistakes.

Thirdly, Priscilla and Aquila "explained the Way of God to him more accurately" (Acts 18:26 NRSV) and expanded his understanding of the kingdom of God. Mentors share information and impart wisdom. Mentors do not make decisions for young leaders, but coach and guide them, enabling them to develop their own leadership skills.

Priscilla's and Aquila's feedback to Apollos illustrates a caring model of mentoring. Their commitment to compassionately coach Apollos proved to be a worthwhile investment in this young leader. Apollos had a teachable heart: He was open to their instruction. They were gifted mentors: Guided by the Holy Spirit, they approached him sensitively and respectfully. Their ability to partner in mentoring increased Apollos' effectiveness as a leader in the Christian community. When Apollos made plans to travel to Achaia, the church at Ephesus sent letters of recommendation, vouching for Apollos and his teaching. We learn later that Apollos emerged as a popular ministry leader in Corinth, the capital of Achaia (see 1 Corinthians 3:4). His effectiveness in Corinth is partly attributed to the mentoring of Priscilla and Aquila.

God allowed me to experience a mentoring moment a while back when God sent me to an "Apollos"—I'll call her April. April had been my student in a graduate program and was a member of a women's ministry team that I was leading. She and I had talked on occasion about her calling into ministry and her vision for leadership. She was applying to another graduate program and asked me to complete a recommendation form. This school was considered to be pretty conservative around women's issues, and she warned me that she had not seen a form like this one with the degree of questions about the applicant's personal life. Even as I read the form, a few categories and questions struck me as particularly intrusive, but I dismissed my concerns.

That is until I had one of the clearest dreams I had had in a long time. In this dream April and I were talking, and I told her that I was receiving a "check in my spirit" about her application. The older folk in my church describe a "check in the spirit" as the Holy Spirit's way of disrupting our peace when we are missing God's cues. Just as Priscilla and Aquila felt led to "show the way more accurately" to Apollos, I eventually felt led to heed this internal prompting and get more information about April's decision.

Mentoring a younger leader is a responsibility that no leader should take lightly. To speak words of guidance into another person's life, to probe into the heart of decisions that are critical to another person's life and livelihood, to listen as a person shares the intimate details of visions, dreams, and passions are all part of the sacred trust that is established between mentor and mentee.

Before I called April, I prayed. Then I listened closely and carefully to her, without judgment. My intent was not to change her mind but to raise some issues that were fundamental to women in ministry. I felt my role was to suggest that she prayerfully weigh these issues as part of her final decision. She listened and was open to my insights. She was not approaching this new environment naïvely, and I was helping her to sort through the issues. She was helping me to see just how mature and Spirit-directed this young woman was. Before we finished our conversation, we prayed together for God's will to be done. I thanked God for April's receptivity, and she thanked me for caring enough to help her gain clarity.

April ultimately chose to attend this school. Wise mentors will always leave their mentees with the freedom to choose and not dictate their actions. April is gifted and her ministry gifts will be a blessing to those to whom she has been and will be sent. But the road to ministry leadership for women is still littered with potholes, and more of us will need to help guide young women around some obstacles and help them remove others as they prepare for ministry leadership.

I believe Priscilla saw "mentoring" as part of her pastoral role in the community of faith over which she and her husband had oversight. Together, she and her co-leader, Aquila, supervised the work of ministry, mentored developing ministry leaders, and organized and led the church. In all of these significant leadership activities, Priscilla is presented as partner in ministry, equally gifted and equally authorized to serve. May Priscilla and Aquila's story inspire you to build leadership partners that advance God's work.

LEADING LESSONS

- Leaders who partner with other leaders to accomplish goals work through conflict and collaborate.
- Leaders who partner respect the gifts, skills, talents, and experiences of the people with whom they collaborate.
- People grow by feedback. No feedback, no growth. Leaders give—and receive—feedback.
- Developing leaders need mentors. Leaders mentor.
- Women and men are equally gifted by God to serve and lead.

REFLECTION AND DISCUSSION QUESTIONS

1. What does it mean for women today to be equal partners with men? At home? At work? In ministry?
2. Is there someone with whom you might want to collaborate to get something done? How might you approach them? What would you like to accomplish?

3. Think of one person who has been a mentor to you. What do you appreciate about the way they helped you?
4. How do you give feedback to others? To your children? To your co-workers? To your friends? How does your church or organization handle giving feedback to its members?
5. Is there someone to whom God is leading you to provide a mentoring moment? In what ways could this person use mentoring right now?

NOTES

SEEING YOURSELF AS A LEADER

1. See Linda Belleville's *Women Leaders and the Church* for an exhaustive study of these roles of women in leadership.

LESSON 1: CREATED TO LEAD

1. "Prostitute Resists Freedom," *Leadership Journal* (Summer 2004), 76.

LESSON 2: THERE IS A BALM IN GILEAD

1. "Daughter of my people" is an idiom used to portray the people of the nations of Judah and Israel. Other idioms include "daughter of Zion" (Isaiah 1:8; Jeremiah 4:31), and "daughter

of Sidon" (Isaiah 23:12). According to the *Dictionary of Biblical Imagery*, "this Hebrew idiom reflects a double metaphor common in the culture of the Ancient Neat East: a capital city was personified by a woman" (p. 194). In this chapter I use "Daughters of Jerusalem" as borrowed from the Song of Solomon 8:4 to capture this ancient custom.

LESSON 4: PUTTING AWAY THE IDOLS
1. Rae Lewis Thornton, *Amazing Grace*, 22.
2. Ibid., 22.
3. Ibid., 15.

LESSON 5: RECOVERING THE QUEEN WITHIN
1. Robert Kegan, *The Evolving Self*, 115-16.
2. Carol Lakey Hess, *Caretakers of Our Common House*, 64.
3. Pat Heim, et al, *In the Company of Women*, 53-54.
4. Ibid., 105.

LESSON 6: STANDING BEFORE MOSES
1. According to Cheryl Sanders, in her "History of Women in the Pentecostal Movement," Susie Stanley, church historian, "uses the term 'stained-glass ceiling' to describe barriers to women's leadership and advancement in Christian denominations with a long history of ordaining them." See Cheryl Sanders, "History of Women in the Pentecostal Movement." *Cyberjournal for Pentecostal-Charismatic Research*, October 1, 1996.
2. Karla G. Bohmbach, "Names and Naming in the Biblical World," in *Women in Scripture*, 33-39.
3. Cheryl Townsend Gilkes, *If It Wasn't for the Women*, 63.
4. Linda Belleville, *Women Leaders and the Church*, 142-143.
5. Much controversy has surrounded Junia. According to Peter Lampei in *The Anchor Bible Dictionary*, it was accepted among the earliest church leaders of antiquity that Junia was a woman and an apostle. It wasn't until the Medieval church that copyist began to write the masculine form of the name in manuscripts,

thus obscuring her gender. According to *The New Interpreter's Bible*, "Junia is thus one of the female "apostles," the only one so called; though presumably others, such as Mary Magdalene, were known as such as well" (p. 762). According to the *New Spirit Filled Life Bible*, "the most likely understanding, and that most common in earliest church exegesis, is . . . Junia [was] part of a husband-wife apostolic team" (Romans 16:7 note, p. 1575).

6. Delores Williams, "A Theology of Advocacy for Women." *Church and Society*, (November/December 2000), 5.

LESSON 7: PAVING THE WAY FOR MINISTRY

1. To protect identities of client organizations, the names of professional colleagues are changed.

2. Linda Belleville, *Women Leaders and the Church: Three Crucial Questions*, 23.

3. Gail R. O'Day, "Acts," in *The Women's Bible Commentary*, 311.

4. Valerie Abrahamsen, "Lydia," in *Women in Scripture*, 110-111.

5. Sue and Larry Richards, *Every Woman in the Bible*, 207.

6. *Chicago Tribune*, December 17, 2003.

7. Laurie Beth Jones, *Jesus, Entrepreneur,* xiii.

LESSON 8: WORKING TOGETHER

1. To protect identities of client organizations, the names of professional colleagues are changed.

REFERENCES

Abrahamsen, Valerie. "Lydia," in *Women in Scripture: A Dictionary of Named and Unnamed Women in the Hebrew Bible, the Apocryphal/Deuterocanonical Books, and the New Testament,* Carol Meyers, gen. ed. Boston: Houghton Mifflin Company, 2000.

Belleville, Linda L. *Women Leaders and the Church: Three Crucial Questions.* Grand Rapids, Mich.: Baker Books, 2000.

Bohmbach, Karla G. "Names and Naming in the Biblical World," in *Women in Scripture: A Dictionary of Named and Unnamed Women in the Hebrew Bible, the Apocryphal/Deuterocanonical Books, and the New Testament,* Carol Meyers, ed. Boston: Houghton Mifflin Company, 2000.

Dictionary of Biblical Imagery, Leland Ryken, James C. Wilhoit, and Tremper Longman III, eds. Downers Grove, Ill.: InterVarsity Press, 1998.

Edelman, Marian Wright. *Lanterns: A Memoir of Mentors*. New York: Perennial, 1999.

Gilkes, Cheryl Townsend. *If It Wasn't for the Women*. Maryknoll, N.Y.: Orbis, 2001.

Heim, Pat, Susan Murphy, with Susan K. Golant. *In the Company of Women: Indirect Aggression among Women: Why We Hurt Each Other and How to Stop*. New York: Jeremy P. Tarcher/ Putnam, 2001.

Hess, Carol Lakey. *Caretakers of Our Common House: Women's Development in Communities of Faith*. Nashville, Tenn.: Abingdon, 1997.

Jones, Laurie Beth. *Jesus, Entrepreneur: Using Ancient Wisdom to Launch and Live Your Dreams*. New York: Three Rivers Press, 2001.

Kegan, Robert. *The Evolving Self: Problems and Process in Human Development*. Cambridge, Mass.: Harvard University Press, 1982.

Lampei, Peter. "Junia," in *The Anchor Bible Dictionary on CD-ROM*, David Noel Freedman, ed. Bantem Oak Harbor, Wash.: Logos Research Systems Inc.; and New York: Doubleday Dell, 1997.

The New Interpreter's Bible, Nashville, Tenn.: Abingdon Press, 2002.

New Spirit Filled Life Bible, Jack W. Hayford, ed. Nashville, Tenn.: Thomas Nelson Bibles, 2002.

O'Day, Gail R. "Acts," in *The Women's Bible Commentary*, Carol A. Newsom and Sharon H. Ringe, eds. Louisville, Ky.: Westminster/John Knox Press, 1992.

"Prostitute Resists Freedom," *Leadership Journal* (Summer 2004):76-77.

Richards, Sue and Larry. *Every Woman in the Bible*. Nashville, Tenn.: Thomas Nelson Publishers, 1999.

Sanders, Cheryl. "History of Women in the Pentecostal Movement." *Cyberjournal for Pentecostal-Charismatic Research*, 1 October 1996, <http://www.fullnet.net/np/archives/cyberj/sanders.html> (17 April 2003).

Thornton, Rae Lewis. *Amazing Grace: Letters along My Journey*. Chicago: Rae Lewis Thornton, Inc., 2004.

Williams, Delores. "A Theology of Advocacy for Women." *Church and Society,* (November/December 2000):4-8.

112507

ABOUT THE AUTHOR

Jeanne Porter is the founder and President of the TransPorter Group in Chicago, where she consults Fortune 500 Companies, churches, community, and government groups. Dr. Porter has served in numerous leadership roles in corporate, educational and religious organizations, and currently serves as the Dean of Ministerial Leadership for the Sacred College of the Pentecostal Assemblies of the World. Dr. Porter is a popular inspirational speaker and conference/retreat leader.

Dr. Porter's writings focus on leadership and leadership development, especially as it relates to women, churches, and communities of color. She is the author of *Leading Ladies: Transformative Biblical Images for Women's Leadership* and a contributing writer to *Women's Liberation: Jesus Style* and *Nature of a Sistuh: Black Women's Lived Experiences in Contemporary Culture*. In addition, she has published numerous articles on transformative leadership development in such venues as *Urban Ministries*, *The African American Pulpit* and *Lutheran Woman Today*. She has also published monographs that explore the dynamics of leadership in the Gullah communities of the Sea Islands.

Dr. Porter received both Bachelor and Master of Science degrees from Ohio State University in Columbus, Ohio, the Doctor of Philosophy in Organizational Communication (with a secondary emphasis in Cultural Studies) from Ohio University in Athens, Ohio, and the Master of Arts of Theological Studies, with a focus on spiritual formation and leadership, from McCormick Theological Seminary, Chicago.